DB2 10.5 DBA for LUW Upgrade from DB2 10.1

Certification Study Notes (Exam 311)

Roger E. Sanders

MC Press Online, LLC
Boise, ID 83703 USA

DB2 10.5 DBA for LUW Upgrade from DB2 10.1: Certification Study Notes (Exam 311)

Roger E. Sanders

First Edition
First Printing—April 2016

MC Press offers excellent discounts on this book when ordered in quantity for bulk purchases or special sales, which may include custom covers and content particular to your business, training goals, marketing focus, and branding interest.

MC Press Online, LLC

Corporate Offices: 3695 W. Quail Heights Court, Boise, ID 83703-3861 USA
Sales and Customer Service: (208) 629-7275 ext. 500;
service@mcpressonline.com
Permissions and Bulk/Special Orders: mcbooks@mcpressonline.com
www.mcpressonline.com • www.mc-store.com

ISBN: 978-1-58347-482-2   WB201604

Dedication

To my good friend and 2015 IBM Fellow, Berni Schiefer

Contents

About the Author

Roger E. Sanders is a DB2 for LUW Offering Manager at IBM and the author of 24 books on relational database technology (23 on DB2 for Linux, UNIX, and Windows; one on ODBC). He has worked with DB2 for Linux, UNIX, and Windows—IBM's relational database management product for open systems—since it was first introduced on the IBM PC as part of OS/2 1.3 Extended Edition (1991), and he has been designing and developing databases and database applications for more than 25 years.

Roger authored a regular column ("Distributed DBA") in *IBM Data Magazine* (formerly *DB2 Magazine*) for 10 years, and he has written numerous tutorials and articles for IBM's developerWorks® website as well as for publications like *Certification Magazine* and *IDUG Solutions Journal* (the official magazine of the International DB2 User's Group). He has delivered a variety of educational seminars and presentations at DB2-related conferences and has participated in the development of 23 DB2 certification exams.

From 2008 to 2015, Roger was recognized as an **IBM Champion** for his contributions to the IBM Data Management community; in 2010 he received recognition as an **IBM developerWorks Contributing Author**, in 2011 as an **IBM developerWorks Professional Author**, and in 2012 as an **IBM developerWorks Master Author, Level 2** for his contributions to the IBM developerWorks community. (Only four individuals worldwide have received this last distinction.) Roger lives in Fuquay-Varina, North Carolina.

Introduction

A few months after the **IBM DB2 10.5 DBA for LUW Upgrade from DB2 10.1** certification exam (Exam 311) was announced (2014), I was contacted by Berni Schiefer and asked if I could develop and present training material on DB2 10.1 and 10.5 to a customer who was interested in moving their entire infrastructure to DB2 10.5 for Linux, UNIX, and Windows. My answer was "yes," and I spent the next three weeks developing training material to cover the 311 certification exam. (I already had training material for DB2 10.1, which is why Berni contacted me to begin with.) And, I used the same technique to develop material for that course that I have used to develop all of my DB2 certification exam preparation courses and study guides—I carefully reviewed notes I had taken during the exam development process, as well as the questions I wrote for that test, and I made sure I covered, in detail, all the objectives that had been defined for that certification exam.

After presenting that material to the customer, I modified it to improve some of the areas I saw class participants struggling to understand, and then I used the updated material to teach a *"DB2 10.5 for Linux, UNIX, and Windows Database Administration Certification Upgrade Exam Preparation"* educational seminar at the 2015 International DB2 User's Group (IDUG) North American Conference. Shortly afterwards, I began to receive emails from individuals seeking a copy of my training material. However, because that material is copyrighted (and is in fact, registered with the U.S. Copyright Office), I don't distribute it freely. Consequently, I was unable to honor their requests.

In January 2016, I was invited to teach my DB2 10.5 DBA certification preparation course at the IDUG conference again. And because I was already working on a new book at the time (the *DB2 10.5 Fundamentals for LUW: Certification Study Guide*), I contacted my publisher and suggested that we make my training material for the 311 exam available, much like we had done before with my training material for the DB2 9.7 DBA certification exam. He agreed, and the result is this book.

If you've bought this book (or if you are thinking about buying this book), chances are you've already decided that you want to acquire the DB2 10.5 for Linux, UNIX, and Windows Database Administrator Certification that's available from IBM. As an individual who has helped develop 23 IBM DB2 certification exams, let me assure you that the exams you must pass in order to become a certified DB2 professional are not easy. IBM prides itself on designing comprehensive certification exams that are relevant to the work environment to which an individual holding a particular certification will be exposed. As a result, all of IBM's certification exams are designed with the following items in mind:

- What are the critical tasks that must be performed by an individual who holds a particular professional certification?
- What skills must an individual possess in order to perform each critical task identified?
- How frequently will an individual perform each critical task identified?

You will find that in order to pass a DB2 certification exam, you must possess a solid understanding of DB2; for some of the more advanced certifications (such as the Advanced DBA exam), you must understand many of DB2's nuances as well.

Now for the good news. You are holding in your hands the *only* material that has been developed specifically to help you prepare for the **DB2 10.5 DBA for LUW Upgrade from DB2 10.1** certification exam (Exam 311). When IBM began work on the 311 exam, I was invited to participate in the exam development process. In addition to helping define the exam objectives, I authored several exam questions, and I provided feedback on many more before the final exams went into production. Consequently, I have seen every exam question you are likely to encounter, and I know every concept you will be tested on when you take the 311 exam. Using this knowledge, I developed these study notes, which cover every concept you must know in order to pass the **DB2 10.5 DBA for LUW Upgrade from DB2 10.1** exam (Exam 311). In addition, you will find, at the end of the book, sample questions that are worded just like the questions on the actual exam. In short, if you see it in this book, count on seeing it on the exam; if you don't see it in this book, it won't be on the exam.

About the IBM Certified Database Administrator—DB2 10.5 DBA for LUW Upgrade from DB2 10.1 Certification

The **IBM Certified Database Administrator—DB2 10.5 DBA for LUW Upgrade from DB2 10.1** certification is designed for experienced DB2 for LUW users who already possess **IBM Certified Database Administrator—DB2 10.1 DBA for Linux, UNIX, and Windows** certification, are knowledgeable about the new features and functions that were introduced with DB2 Version 10.5, and are capable of performing the tasks required to administer DB2 10.5 for LUW instances and databases.

Candidates who obtained **IBM Certified Database Administrator—DB2 10.1 for Linux, UNIX, and Windows** certification by taking (and passing) either the *DB2 9 Family Fundamentals exam* (Exam 730), the *DB2 10.1 Fundamentals* exam (Exam 610), or the *DB2 10.5 Fundamentals for LUW* exam (Exam

615) *and* the *DB2 10.1 DBA for Linux, UNIX, and Windows* exam
(Exam 611) can acquire **IBM Certified Database Administrator—
DB2 10.5 DBA for LUW Upgrade from DB2 10.1** certification by
taking (and passing) the *DB2 10.5 DBA for LUW Upgrade from DB2
10.1* exam (Exam 311). Figure 1 displays the road map for acquiring
**IBM Certified Database Administrator—DB2 10.5 DBA for
LUW Upgrade from DB2 10.1** certification.

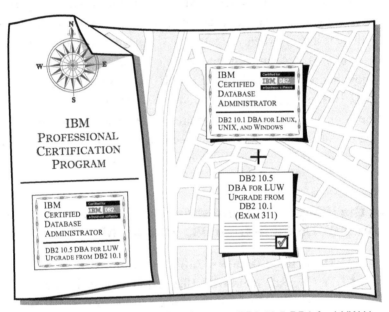

*Figure 1: IBM Certified Database Administrator—DB2 10.5 DBA for LUW Upgrade
from DB2 10.1 certification road map*

Conventions Used

Many examples of DB2 administrative commands and SQL
statements can be found throughout this book. The following
conventions are used whenever a DB2 command or SQL statement is
presented:

[ ]   Parameters or items shown inside of brackets are required and must be provided.

< >   Parameters or items shown inside of angle brackets are optional and do not have to be provided.

| Vertical bars are used to indicate that one (and only one) item in the list of items presented can be specified

,...   A comma followed by three periods (ellipsis) indicate that multiple instances of the preceding parameter or item can be included in the DB2 command or SQL statement

The following example illustrates each of these conventions:

Example

```
UPDATE [DATABASE | DB]
[CONFIGURATION | CONFIG | CFG]
FOR [DatabaseAlias]
USING [[KeyWord] [Value] ,...]
<IMMEDIATE | DEFERRED>
```

In this example, DATABASE or DB is required, as is CONFIGURATION, CONFIG, or CFG, a *DatabaseAlias* value, and a *Keyword-Value* pair, as indicated by the brackets ([ ]). In the case of DATABASE or DB, only one option can be specified, as indicated by the vertical bar (|). The same is true for CONFIGURATION, CONFIG, or CFG. More than one *KeyWord-Value* pair can be provided, as indicated by the comma-ellipsis (,...) characters that follow the *Value* parameter. IMMEDIATE and DEFERRED are optional, as indicated by the angle brackets (< >), and either one or the other can be specified, but not both, as indicated by the vertical bar (|).

SQL is not a case-sensitive language, but for clarity, the examples provided are shown in mixed case—command syntax is presented in upper case while user-supplied elements such as table names and column names are presented in lower case. However, the examples shown can be entered in any case.

Note: Although basic syntax is presented for most of the SQL statements covered in this book, the actual syntax supported can be much more complex. To view the complete syntax for a specific DB2 command or SQL statement or to obtain more information about a particular command or statement, refer to the *IBM DB2 10.5 Knowledge Center*.

1

DB2 10.5 Overview

A brief overview of some of the new features and functionality introduced with DB2 10.5 for Linux, UNIX, and Windows.

DB2 10.5 With BLU Acceleration Design Principles

DB2 10.5 with BLU Acceleration was designed around the following seven "big ideas":

1. Simple to implement and use

- *"It's just DB2 and standard SQL"*
- *Load data and start getting the performance gains of DB2 with BLU Acceleration immediately*

2. Compute-friendly encoding and compression

- *"Always on" compression with approximate Huffman encoding*
- *Encoded values do not need to be decompressed during evaluation*

3. Multiply the power of the CPU

- *Takes advantage of special hardware instructions to work on multiple data elements with a single instruction (SIMD)*

DB2 10.5 With BLU Acceleration Design Principles (Continued)

4. Column data store

- *Minimal I/O*
  - I/O is only performed on the columns and values that match query predicates
  - As queries progress through a pipeline, the working set of pages is reduced
- *Work performed directly on columns*
  - Predicates, joins, scans, etc. all work on individual columns
  - Rows are not materialized until absolutely necessary to build a result data set
- *Improved memory density*
  - Columnar data is kept compressed in memory
- *Extreme compression*
  - More data values can be packed into a very small amount of memory or disk space
- *Cache efficiency*
  - Data is packed into cache-friendly structures

DB2 10.5 With BLU Acceleration Design Principles (Continued)

5. Core-friendly parallelism

- *Designed to take advantage of the cores available and to always drive multi-core parallelism when processing queries*
- *Maximizes CPU cache*

6. Scan-friendly memory caching

- *New algorithms cache data in RAM more effectively*
- *Higher percentage of interesting data fits in memory*
- *Enhanced caching strategy improves buffer pool utilization*

7. Data skipping

- *Automatic detection and avoidance of large sections of data that is not needed to resolve a query*
- *Order of magnitude savings in I/O, RAM, and CPU*
- *No user action required to define or use – truly invisible*

What Else Is New In DB2 10.5?

In addition to BLU Acceleration, DB2 10.5 offers the following new features and functionality:

- ❖ Simplified product packaging
- ❖ Simplified Fix Pack installs
- ❖ Enhanced tooling
- ❖ Extended row size support
- ❖ Expression-based indexes
- ❖ Ability to exclude NULL index keys
- ❖ NOT ENFORCED primary keys and unique constraints
- ❖ DB2 Advanced Copy Services (ACS) scripting for snapshot backup and restore operations

What Else Is New In DB2 10.5? (Continued)

- ❖ Online topology changes to DB2 pureScale clusters
- ❖ Explicit hierarchical locking in DB2 pureScale environments
- ❖ Workload balancing on subsets of DB2 pureScale members (multi-tenancy)
- ❖ In-place table REORGs in DB2 pureScale environments
- ❖ Member-specific self-tuning memory manager (STMM) in DB2 pureScale environments
- ❖ Mobility of backup images between DB2 10.5 Enterprise Server Edition and DB2 pureScale
- ❖ Support for HADR in DB2 pureScale environments

2

DB2 Server Management

Seventeen percent (17%) of the DB2 10.5 Database Administration for LUW Upgrade Exam (Exam 311) is designed to test your knowledge of basic DB2 10.5 server management.

Servers, Instances, and Databases

DB2 for Linux, UNIX, and Windows (otherwise known as DB2 for LUW) sees the world as a hierarchy of objects. *Servers* occupy the highest level of this hierarchy, *instances* occupy the second level, and *databases* make up the third.

DB2 Servers, Instances, and Databases – Illustrated

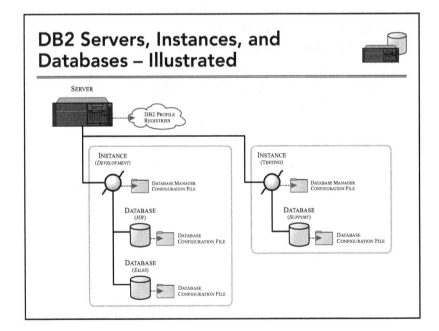

Configuring The DB2 Server Environment

The behavior of a DB2 server is controlled, in part, by a collection of environment variables, whose values are stored in the following *profile registries*:

❖ The DB2 Global Level Profile Registry
❖ The DB2 Instance Level Profile Registry
❖ The DB2 Instance Node Level Profile Registry

The contents of each of these profile registries can be examined using the **db2set** command; this command is also used to assign values to profile registry variables.

Configuring DB2 Instances

The behavior of a DB2 instance is controlled, in part, by a special configuration file. This file consists of several different parameters; the values assigned to each parameter can be viewed or altered using the following commands:

❖ **GET DATABASE MANAGER CONFIGURATION**
❖ **UPDATE DATABASE MANAGER CONFIGURATION**
❖ **RESET DATABASE MANAGER CONFIGURATION**

Configuring DB2 Databases

As with DB2 instances, the behavior of a DB2 database is controlled, in part, by a special configuration file. This file consists of more than 100 different parameters and the value assigned to each parameter can be viewed or modified using the following commands:

- ❖ **GET DATABASE CONFIGURATION**
- ❖ **UPDATE DATABASE CONFIGURATION**
- ❖ **RESET DATABASE CONFIGURATION**

Configuring a DB2 10.5 Database Environment For BLU Acceleration

The easiest way to configure a DB2 10.5 database environment for BLU Acceleration is by assigning the value **ANALYTICS** to the **DB2_WORKLOAD** registry variable *before* any databases are created. For example:

```
db2set DB2_WORKLOAD=ANALYTICS
```

Assigns appropriate values to a set of configuration parameters to enable DB2 10.5 BLU Acceleration

Behavior When DB2_WORKLOAD Is Set To ANALYTICS

When the **DB2_WORKLOAD** registry variable is assigned the value **ANALYTICS**:

* The *dft_table_org* (default table organization for user tables) database configuration parameter is set to **COLUMN**.
* The *dft_degree* (default degree of intrapartition parallelism) database configuration parameter is set to **ANY**.
* The *pagesize* (default database page size) database configuration parameter is set to **32** KB.
* The *dft_extent_sz* (default extent size) database configuration parameter is set to **4**.

Behavior When DB2_WORKLOAD Is Set To ANALYTICS (Continued)

* The *intra_parallel* (use intrapartition query parallelism) database manager configuration parameter is set to **YES**. (*Intrapartition parallelism is turned on at the instance level; however, this behavior does not take effect until the instance is stopped and restarted.*)
* The values of the *sortheap* (sort heap) and *sheapthres_shr* (sort heap threshold for shared sorts) database configuration parameters are calculated and set specifically for an analytics workload.
* The *util_heap_sz* (utility heap size) database configuration parameter is set to a value that takes into account the additional memory that is required to load data into column-organized tables.

Behavior When DB2_WORKLOAD Is Set To ANALYTICS (Continued)

❖ The *auto_reorg* (automatic reorganization) database configuration parameter is set to **ON**.

❖ A default space reclamation policy is installed and automatic table maintenance is configured so that empty extents are automatically returned to table space storage for reuse whenever data is deleted from column-organized tables.

Prerequisites For Creating BLU Acceleration Databases

Once the value **ANALYTICS** has been assigned to the **DB2_WORKLOAD** registry variable:

❖ Only single-partition databases can be created.

❖ All databases must use the UNICODE code set and IDENTITY collation.

❖ The *auto_runstats* (automatic table RUNSTATS operations) database configuration parameter must be set to **OFF**.*

❖ The *util_heap_sz* (utility heap size) database configuration parameter should be set to at least **1,000,000** pages or assigned the value **AUTOMATIC**.

This was required initially, but is no longer.

DB2 Workload Manager

DB2 Workload Manager (WLM) is a comprehensive workload management feature that can help identify, manage, and control database workloads (applications, users, and so on) so that database server throughput and resource utilization are maximized.

WLM is designed to limit the number of disruptive activities that can run concurrently and to stop the execution of activities that exceed predefined boundaries.

DB2 Workload Manager Objects

The DB2 Workload Manager architecture consists of the following objects:

❖ Service classes

A service class acts as a unique execution environment for any grouping of work that you can assign resources to, control, and monitor.

❖ Workloads

A workload is an object that is used to identify submitted database work or a user connection so it can be managed.

❖ Thresholds

A threshold is an object that sets a predefined limit over specific criteria, such as the consumption of a specific resource or duration of time.

DB2 Workload Manager Objects (Continued)

❖ Work action sets

> *A work action set is an object that dictates what is to happen when the work of interest is detected.*

❖ Work class sets

> *A work class set is an object that defines the characteristics of the work of interest.*

❖ Histogram templates

> *A histogram is a graphical display of tabulated frequencies; a histogram template is an object with no predefined measurement units that is used to specify what a histogram should look like.*

WLM Objects That Aid In Concurrency Control

To aid in concurrency control, the following default workload management objects are created automatically for new (or upgraded) DB2 10.5 databases:

❖ A **SYSDEFAULTMANAGEDSUBCLASS** service subclass (under the SYSDEFAULTUSERCLASS superclass)

> *The service subclass where heavyweight queries against column-organized tables run and can be controlled and monitored as a group.*

WLM Objects That Aid In Concurrency Control (Continued)

❖ A **SYSDEFAULTCONCURRENT** threshold (under the CONCURRENTDBCOORDACTIVITIES threshold)

The threshold that is applied to the SYSDEFAULTMANAGEDSUBCLASS subclass to control the number of concurrently running queries that are running in that subclass.

The threshold on the SYSDEFAULTMANAGEDSUBCLASS service subclass is enabled by default for newly created databases only.

❖ A **SYSMANAGEDQUERIES** work class and a **SYSDEFAULTUSERWCS** work class set

The work class and work class set that identify the class of heavyweight queries to control.

WLM Objects That Aid In Concurrency Control (Continued)

❖ A **SYSMAPMANAGEDQUERIES** work action and a **SYSDEFAULTUSERWAS** work action set

The work action and work action set that maps all queries that fall into the SYSMANAGEDQUERIES work class to the SYSDEFAULTMANAGEDSUBCLASS service subclass.

The SYSDEFAULTUSERWAS work action set is enabled by default so that queries that meet the criteria specified for the SYSMANAGEDQUERIES work class run in the SYSDEFAULTMANAGEDSUBCLASS service subclass.

DB2 Warehouse

DB2 Warehouse is a suite of products that combines the strength of DB2 with a data warehousing infrastructure; the following components are provided in DB2 Warehouse:

❖ DB2 Warehouse Data Server
❖ DB2 Warehouse Application Server
❖ DB2 Warehouse Client

New Functionality In The SQL Warehousing Tool (SQW)

Starting with DB2 10.5, the following features are available with the SQL Warehousing Tool (SQW) component of the DB2 Warehouse Client:

❖ BLU Acceleration support
❖ Oracle-compatibility mode support
❖ Secure Shell (SSH) protocol support in the Administration Console
❖ Ability to establish a secure connection without a password in Design Studio

3

Physical Design

Thirty-seven percent (37%) of the DB2 10.5 Database Administration for LUW Upgrade Exam (Exam 311) is designed to test your ability to use many of the new features that were introduced with DB2 10.5.

Table Spaces

Table spaces are used to control where data for a database is physically stored and to provide a layer of indirection between database objects (i.e., tables, indexes, etc.) and the storage containers where an object's data resides. Two types of table spaces exist:

- ❖ System Managed Space (SMS)*
- ❖ Database Managed Space (DMS)*

The ability to explicitly define SMS table spaces for permanent data storage was deprecated in DB2 10.1; the ability to explicitly define DMS table spaces for permanent data storage was deprecated in DB2 10.1, Fix Pack 1.

Automatic Storage Table Spaces

If a database is using automatic storage, another type of table space known as an *automatic storage* (AS) table space can exist*. Automatic storage table spaces are an extension of SMS and DMS table spaces:

- ❖ *Regular* and *large* automatic storage table spaces are created as auto-resizing DMS table spaces (that use files for containers)
- ❖ *Temporary* automatic storage table spaces are created as SMS table spaces (that use directories for containers)

Column-organized tables can only be created in automatic storage table spaces.

The Traditional Approach To Database Storage

Traditionally, storage for DB2 databases has been managed at the table space level, using explicit SMS and DMS table space container definitions. But there are some disadvantages to this approach:

❖ When DMS table spaces are used, the DBA is responsible for extending or adding containers to them whenever additional space is required; consequently, storage space consumption must be closely monitored

❖ When SMS table spaces are used, the operating system automatically grows them as space is consumed; but, the overhead of using SMS table spaces has an impact on performance

The Traditional Approach To Database Storage – Illustrated

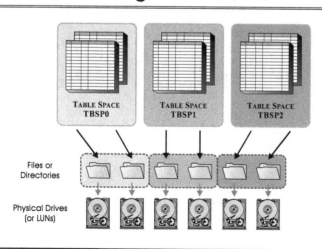

Automatic Storage Databases

Automatic storage databases make storage management easier. Instead of relying on a DBA to manage storage at the table space level using explicit container definitions, the DB2 database manager is responsible for managing storage at the database level, creating, extending or adding containers as needed, to support table space growth.

Automatic Storage Databases – Illustrated

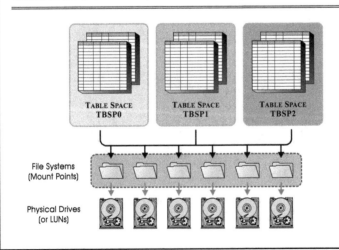

Tables

In a relational database, a table represents a set of data values that have been organized into vertical *columns* (or *fields*) and horizontal *rows* (or *records*); where a row and column intersect is referred to as a *value* (or *cell*).

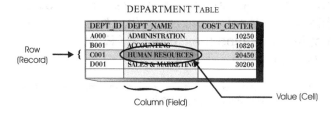

DEPARTMENT TABLE

DEPT_ID	DEPT_NAME	COST_CENTER
A000	ADMINISTRATION	10250
B001	ACCOUNTING	10820
C001	HUMAN RESOURCES	20450
D001	SALES & MARKETING	30200

Row (Record)

Column (Field)

Value (Cell)

Extended Row Size Support

Normally, records in a table are organized into pages that are **4**, **8**, **16**, or **32** KB in length. And prior to DB2 10.5, the maximum number of bytes allowed in a single row was dependent upon the page size of the table space being used to store the table – an attempt to create a table with a row length that exceeded the maximum length allowed by the underlying table space would result in an error.

With DB2 10.5's *extended row size support*, it is now possible to create a table whose row length exceeds the underlying table space's page size.

Enabling Extended Row Size Support

Extended row size support is enabled by assigning the value **ENABLE** to the *extended_row_sz* database configuration parameter.

Once this assignment has been made, a table whose row length exceeds the maximum length allowed by the underlying table space can be created – provided the table has at least one column that has a varying-length string data type (i.e., **VARCHAR** or **VARGRAPHIC**)*.

*To take advantage of extended row size support, a table **must** have at least one column with a varying-length string data type.

How Extended Row Size Support Is Implemented

If extended row size support is enabled, whenever a row is inserted or updated in a table and the physical length of the data for the row exceeds the maximum record length allowed (by the underlying table space), a subset of the data stored in a varying-length string column is moved out of the row and stored as large object (LOB) data.

It's important to note that when this happens, the varying-length string column's data type does not change (i.e., the column's data type is not converted to **CLOB** or **DBCLOB**).

Column-Organized Tables

The most prominent feature found in DB2 10.5 is a new, in-memory columnar table type. Unlike row-organized tables, which store data for complete records (rows) in pages and extents, column-organized tables store data for *individual columns* in pages and extents.

Storing data by column reduces the amount of I/O needed to process workloads that consist of complex queries (which are commonly characterized by multi-table joins, grouping, aggregation, and table scans).

How Row-Organized Table Data Is Stored

EMPLOYEE TABLE

FIRST	LAST	PHONE	ADDRESS	CITY	STATE	ZIP
Rebecca	Geyer	(413) 555-1357	18 Main Street	Springfield	MA	01111
Mark	Hayakawa	(415) 555-2468	1020 Lombard Street	San Francisco	CA	94109
Bryan	Boone	(567) 555-9876	911 Elm Street	Toledo	OH	43601
James	Coleman	(415) 555-5432	2318 Hyde Street	San Francisco	CA	94104
Linda	Bookman	(408) 555-9753	1017 Milton Avenue	San Jose	CA	95141
Robert	Jancer	(971) 555-1357	2009 Elk Lane	Beaverton	OR	97075
Andy	Watson	(408) 555-2468	1017 Chestnut Street	San Jose	CA	95141
Susan	Boodie	(919) 555-1212	5661 Blount Street	Raleigh	NC	27605
Dorian	Naveh	(520) 555-8642	2120 Bank Street	Tucson	AZ	85701
Jane	Esposito	(669) 555-4996	2120 Oak Street	Santa Clara	CA	95051

PAGE →

Rebecca	Geyer	(413) 555-1357	18 Main Street	Springfield	MA	01111
Mark	Hayakawa	(415) 555-2468	1020 Lombard Street	San Francisco	CA	94109
Bryan	Boone	(567) 555-9876	911 Elm Street	Toledo	OH	43601

PAGE →

James	Coleman	(415) 555-5432	2318 Hyde Street	San Francisco	CA	94104
Linda	Bookman	(408) 555-9753	1017 Milton Avenue	San Jose	CA	95141
Robert	Jancer	(971) 555-1357	2009 Elk Lane	Beaverton	OR	97075

PAGE →

Andy	Watson	(408) 555-2468	1017 Chestnut Street	San Jose	CA	95141
Susan	Boodie	(919) 555-1212	5661 Blount Street	Raleigh	NC	27605
Dorian	Naveh	(520) 555-8642	2120 Bank Street	Tucson	AZ	85701

PAGE →

Jane	Esposito	(669) 555-4996	2120 Oak Street	Santa Clara	CA	95051

How Column-Organized Table Data Is Stored

EMPLOYEE TABLE

FIRST	LAST	PHONE	ADDRESS	CITY	STATE	ZIP
Rebecca	Geyer	(413) 555-1357	18 Main Street	Springfield	MA	01111
Mark	Hayakawa	(415) 555-2468	1020 Lombard Street	San Francisco	CA	94109
Bryan	Boone	(567) 555-9876	911 Elm Street	Toledo	OH	43601
James	Coleman	(415) 555-5432	2318 Hyde Street	San Francisco	CA	94104
Linda	Bookman	(408) 555-9753	1017 Milton Avenue	San Jose	CA	95141
Robert	Jancer	(971) 555-1357	2009 Elk Lane	Beaverton	OR	97075
Andy	Watson	(408) 555-2468	1017 Chestnut Street	San Jose	CA	95141
Susan	Boodie	(919) 555-1212	5661 Blount Street	Raleigh	NC	27605
Dorian	Naveh	(520) 555-8642	2120 Bank Street	Tucson	AZ	85701
Jane	Esposito	(669) 555-4996	2120 Oak Street	Santa Clara	CA	95051

Tuple Sequence Number (TSN)

TSN							
000	Rebecca	Geyer	(413) 555-1357	18 Main Street	Springfield	MA	01111
001	Mark	Hayakawa	(415) 555-2468	1020 Lombard Street	San Francisco	CA	94109
002	Bryan	Boone	(567) 555-9876	911 Elm Street	Toledo	OH	43601
003	James	Coleman	(415) 555-5432	2318 Hyde Street	San Francisco	CA	94104
004	Linda	Bookman	(408) 555-9753	1017 Milton Avenue	San Jose	CA	95141
005	Robert	Jancer	(971) 555-1357	2009 Elk Lane	Beaverton	OR	97075
006	Andy	Watson	(408) 555-2468	1017 Chestnut Street	San Jose	CA	95141
007	Susan	Boodie	(919) 555-1212	5661 Blount Street	Raleigh	NC	27605
008	Dorian	Naveh	(520) 555-8642	2120 Bank Street	Tucson	AZ	85701
009	Jane	Esposito	(669) 555-4996	2120 Oak Street	Santa Clara	CA	95051
010							
011							
012							
...							

← PAGE*

Separate set of pages and extents for each column

← PAGE*

Other Differences Between Row and Column-Organized Tables

Other ways in which column-organized tables differ from row-organized tables include:

* ❖ Indexes are not needed (nor can they be created)
* ❖ **REORG**s do not have to be manually performed (they're done automatically)
* ❖ Multidimensional clustering (MDC) is not needed (nor is it allowed)
* ❖ Materialized query tables (MQTs), materialized views, and statistical views are not needed (nor are they allowed)
* ❖ Table partitioning is not supported

Creating Column-Organized Tables

Column-organized tables can be created by executing the **CREATE TABLE** statement with the **ORGANIZE BY COLUMN** clause specified.

If you want to create column-organized tables without having to specify the **ORGANIZE BY COLUMN** clause, you can set the default table organization type to column-organized by assigning the value **COLUMN** to the *dft_table_org* database configuration parameter before tables are created*.

*When the value **ANALYTICS** *is assigned to the* **DB2_WORKLOAD** *registry variable, the value* **COLUMN** *is automatically assigned to the* *dft_table_org* *database configuration parameter.*

CREATE TABLE (Column-Organized) Example

```
CREATE TABLE employee
  (empid    INTEGER,
   name     VARCHAR(50),
   hiredate DATE)
ORGANIZE BY COLUMN
IN userspace2
```

Creates a column-organized table named EMPLOYEE that has three columns and that resides in a table space named USERSPACE2

When Should Column-Organized Tables Be Used?

When the majority of database workloads are entirely analytical or OLAP in nature, the recommended approach is to put as many tables as possible into column-organized format.

(Analytical and OLAP workloads are typically characterized by nonselective data access – usually involving more than 5% of the data – and extensive scanning, grouping, and aggregation.)

When Should Row-Organized Tables Be Used?

When the majority of database workloads are transactional in nature, it is recommended that traditional row-organized tables (with index access) be used; *here, the use of column-organized tables should be avoided.*

In addition, if the **DB2_COMPATIBILITY_VECTOR** registry variable has been assigned the value **ORA** (to enable Oracle-compatibility), traditional row-organized tables *must* be used; the use of column-organized tables with Oracle-compatibility is not supported.

Using Row-Organized and Column-Organized Tables Together

Column-organized tables and row-organized tables can coexist in the same database, the same schema, and/or the same table space; they can also be accessed by the same query.

For mixed workloads, which include a combination of analytic query processing and very selective data access (involving less than 2% of the data), it can be beneficial to use a mixture of row-organized and column-organized tables, as opposed to just one table type.

Limitations On Referencing Column-Organized Tables

In most cases, column-organized tables can be referenced in the same way that row-organized tables can. For example, both types of tables can serve as the source or target of a view – provided the view is not created with the **WITH CHECK OPTION** clause specified.

There are some instances, however, where column-organized tables cannot be used. For example, they cannot be referenced as the source or target of an index, a trigger, or a nickname.

A Word About Materialized Query Tables (MQTs)

Materialized query tables (MQTs) are tables whose definition is based on the results of a query.

MQTs are similar to views in that their data comes from one or more base tables. Where they differ is in the way their data is generated and where that data is stored – MQT data is generated by executing the query upon which the MQT is based, either at regular intervals or at a specific point in time that is dictated by the user. And MQT data physically resides in the MQT itself, rather than in the MQT's underlying base table(s).

Shadow Tables

A shadow table is a column-organized copy of one or more columns of a row-organized table; shadow tables are implemented as MQTs that are maintained by replication.

Introduced in DB2 10.5, FixPack 4, shadow tables offer a way to get the query performance benefits provided by BLU Acceleration in an online transaction processing (OLTP) environment.

Indexes

An index is an object that contains a set of pointers that are logically ordered by the values of one or more keys; typically, the pointers refer to rows in a row-organized table, blocks in an multidimensional clustering table (MDC) or insert time clustering (ITC) table, or pattern expressions in an XML document.

In DB2 10.5, index pointers can also refer to the results of a user-supplied expression.

Expression-Based Indexes

An expression-based index is an index whose key is derived from some type of expression (for instance, a scalar function).

Expression-based indexes are best suited for queries that contain some type of column expression; the performance of such queries can often be greatly improved if the DB2 optimizer can choose an access plan that uses an index on the same expression.

Creating Expression-Based Indexes

Expression-based indexes are created by executing the **CREATE INDEX** statement with one or more expressions specified. For example:

```
CREATE UNIQUE* INDEX emp_name_idx
  ON employee(UPPER(name))
```

Creates a unique expression-based index named EMP_NAME_IDX whose key values consist of values retrieved from a column named NAME in a table named EMPLOYEE that have been converted to upper case

*When the **UNIQUE** clause is specified in the **CREATE INDEX** statement used to create an expression-based index, uniqueness will be enforced against the values stored in the index – not the values stored in the associated table.*

Expression-Based Index Supporting Objects

When an expression-based index is created, two supporting objects are created as well: *a system-generated package* and *a system-generated statistical view*.

The package is used to generate key values while the statistical view is used for statistics collection – when the **RUNSTATS** command is issued against a table for which one or more expression-based indexes have been defined, statistics for the expression-based keys are collected and stored in the corresponding statistical view.

Excluding NULL Index Keys

Starting with DB2 10.5, NULL key values can be excluded from indexes; excluding NULL keys can result in storage savings and improved performance, particularly in cases where queries do not need (or want) to access data associated with a NULL key.

Creating Indexes That Exclude NULL Key Values

An index for which entries will not be made when all parts of the index key contain the NULL value can be created by executing a **CREATE INDEX** statement with the **EXCLUDE NULL KEYS** clause specified. For example:

```
CREATE UNIQUE* INDEX dept_idx
  ON department(dept_id)
  EXCLUDE NULL KEYS
```

Creates a unique index named DEPT_IDX that does not store NULL key column values

*If such an index is defined as being unique, rows with NULL key values are not used to enforce uniqueness.

Constraints

Constraints are rules that govern how data values can be added to a base table*, as well as how existing data values can be modified. The following types of constraints are available with DB2:

- ❖ NOT NULL constraints
- ❖ Default constraints
- ❖ Check constraints
- ❖ Unique constraints
- ❖ Referential Integrity constraints
- ❖ Informational constraints

*Constraints cannot be defined for views or system catalog tables.

Informational Constraints

An informational constraint is a constraint that is used to provide the DB2 optimizer with information that may help improve query performance but *that is not enforced*.

Traditionally, informational constraints have been defined by appending the keywords **NOT ENFORCED** to check and referential integrity constraint definitions.

Informational Constraint – Illustrated

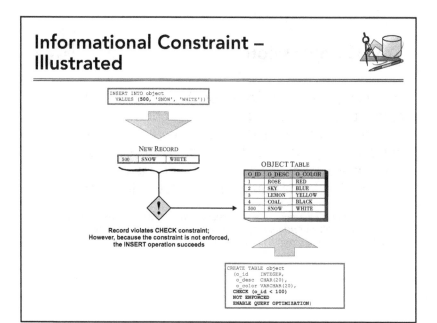

```
INSERT INTO object
    VALUES (500, 'SNOW', 'WHITE'))
```

NEW RECORD

| 500 | SNOW | WHITE |

OBJECT TABLE

O_ID	O_DESC	O_COLOR
1	ROSE	RED
2	SKY	BLUE
3	LEMON	YELLOW
4	COAL	BLACK
500	SNOW	WHITE

Record violates CHECK constraint;
However, because the constraint is not enforced,
the INSERT operation succeeds

```
CREATE TABLE object
    (o_id    INTEGER,
     o_desc  CHAR(20),
     o_color VARCHAR(20),
     CHECK (o_id < 100)
     NOT ENFORCED
     ENABLE QUERY OPTIMIZATION)
```

Informational (NOT ENFORCED) Primary Key and Unique Constraints

Prior to DB2 10.5, only check and referential integrity constraints could be created as informational constraints.

However, starting with DB2 10.5, primary key and unique informational constraints can be created as well. These types of informational constraints help the DB2 optimizer select an optimal access plan to use when index access to data doesn't provide any additional benefit*.

While indexes cannot be created for column-organized tables, informational primary keys and informational unique constraints can.

Row Compression

Row compression is based on the principle that large amounts of data tend to be highly redundant. It is applied by searching for repeating patterns in the data and replacing those patterns with 12-bit symbols, which are stored along with the patterns they represent in a table-level or page-level dictionary*.

*Compression dictionaries are stored, along with compressed data, in the corresponding table or page; they are loaded into memory and used to uncompress the data when it is accessed.

Row Compression Methods

Two methods of row compression are available:

* ❖ Classic row compression*

    There is only one table-level compression dictionary for each table that gets compressed; this dictionary contains a mapping of patterns that frequently occur in rows throughout the table.

* ❖ Adaptive row compression

    There can be one table-level compression dictionary and multiple page-level compression dictionaries for each table that gets compressed; each page-level dictionary contains a mapping of patterns that frequently occur in rows throughout a single page.

*When a database is converted to DB2 10.5, existing compressed tables will have classic row compression enabled; current and future records will be compressed at the table level.

Classic Row Compression – Illustrated

EMPLOYEE Table

FIRST	LAST	PHONE	ADDRESS	CITY	STATE	ZIP
Rebecca	Geyer	(415) 555-1357	1020 Lombard Street	San Francisco	CA	94109
Mark	Hayakawa	(415) 555-2468	1020 Lombard Street	San Francisco	CA	94109
Bryan	Boone	(415) 555-9876	2318 Hyde Street	San Francisco	CA	94104
James	Coleman	(415) 555-5432	2318 Hyde Street	San Francisco	CA	94104
Linda	Bookman	(408) 555-9753	1017 Chestnut Street	San Jose	CA	95141
Robert	Jancer	(408) 555-1357	1017 Chestnut Street	San Jose	CA	95141
Andy	Watson	(408) 555-2468	1017 Chestnut Street	San Jose	CA	95141
Susan	Boodie	(408) 555-1212	1017 Chestnut Street	San Jose	CA	95141

Rebecca	Geyer	(415) 555-1357	1020 Lombard (2)	(3) (4)	(6)	4109
Mark	Hayakawa	(415) 555-2468	1020 Lombard (2)	(3) (4)	(6)	4109
Bryan	(1)ne	(415) 555-9876	2318 Hyde (2)	(3) (4)	(6)	4104
James	Coleman	(415) 555-5432	2318 Hyde (2)	(3) (4)	(6)	4104
Linda	(1)man	(408) 555-9753	1017 Chestnut (2)	(3) (5)	(6)	5141
Robert	Jancer	(408) 555-1357	1017 Chestnut (2)	(3) (5)	(6)	5141
Andy	Watson	(408) 555-2468	1017 Chestnut (2)	(3) (5)	(6)	5141
Susan	(1)die	(408) 555-1212	1017 Chestnut (2)	(3) (5)	(6)	5141

COMPRESSED DATA ROWS

1	Boo
2	Street
3	San
4	Francisco
5	Jose
6	CA 9

TABLE-LEVEL COMPRESSION DICTIONARY

Adaptive Row Compression – Illustrated

TABLE-LEVEL COMPRESSED DATA PAGE 1

Rebecca	Geyer	(415) 555-1357	1020 Lombard (2)	(3) (4)	(6)	4109
Mark	Hayakawa	(415) 555-2468	1020 Lombard (2)	(3) (4)	(6)	4109
Bryan	(1)ne	(415) 555-9876	2318 Hyde (2)	(3) (4)	(6)	4104
James	Coleman	(415) 555-5432	2318 Hyde (2)	(3) (4)	(6)	4104

Rebecca	Geyer	(1) 1357	(2)
Mark	Hayakawa	(1) 2468	(2)
Bryan	[1]ne	(1) 9876	(3)
James	Coleman	(1) 5432	(3)

COMPRESSED DATA PAGE 1

1	(415) 555-
2	1020 Lombard [2] [3] [4] [6] 4109
3	2318 Hyde [2] [3] [4] [6] 4104

PAGE-LEVEL COMPRESSION DICTIONARY

TABLE-LEVEL COMPRESSED DATA PAGE 2

Linda	(1)man	(408) 555-9753	1017 Chestnut (2)	(3) (5)	(6)	5141
Robert	Jancer	(408) 555-1357	1017 Chestnut (2)	(3) (5)	(6)	5141
Andy	Watson	(408) 554-2468	1017 Chestnut (2)	(3) (5)	(6)	5141
Susan	(1)die	(408) 554-1212	1017 Chestnut (2)	(3) (5)	(6)	5141

Linda	[1]man	(1) 9753	(3)
Robert	Jancer	(1) 1357	(3)
Andy	Watson	(2) 2468	(3)
Susan	[1]die	(2) 1212	(3)

COMPRESSED DATA PAGE 2

1	(408) 555-
2	(408) 554-
3	1017 Chestnut [2] [3] [5] [6] 5141

PAGE-LEVEL COMPRESSION DICTIONARY

Enabling A Table For Compression

Before data in a table can be compressed, the table must be "enabled" for compression; this is done by executing one of the following statements:

* ❖ **CREATE TABLE ...**
  COMPRESS YES <ADAPTIVE* | STATIC>
* ❖ **ALTER TABLE ...**
  COMPRESS YES <ADAPTIVE* | STATIC>

*When a table is enabled for adaptive compression, the entire table is enabled, even if it is a partitioned table that consists of multiple data partitions.

Enabling An Index For Compression

Similarly, before data in an index can be compressed, the index must be enabled for compression; this is done by executing one of the following statements:

* ❖ **CREATE INDEX ... COMPRESS YES**
* ❖ **ALTER INDEX [*IndexName*] COMPRESS YES**

Index compression is automatically enabled for compressed tables* and automatically disabled for uncompressed tables.

*When an index is created on a table that has been enabled for compression, the index is enabled for compression, by default.

Index Compression Restrictions

The following types of indexes can NOT be enabled for compression:

- ❖ Multidimensional clustering (MDC) block indexes
- ❖ Insert time clustering (ITC) block indexes
- ❖ Catalog indexes
- ❖ XML indexes
- ❖ Indexes on created global temporary tables
- ❖ Indexes on declared global temporary tables

Column-Organized Table Compression

Column-organized tables are automatically compressed using what is known as *approximate Huffman encoding.*

With this form of compression (referred to as *actionable compression*), values that appear more frequently are compressed at a higher level than values that do not appear as often. Once encoded, data is packed as tightly as possible in a collection of bits that equal the register width of the CPU of the server being used, resulting in fewer I/Os, better memory utilization, and fewer CPU cycles to process.

Huffman Encoding – Illustrated

Letter	Probability	Huffman Code
A	0.154	1
B	0.110	01
C	0.072	0010
D	0.063	0011
E	0.059	0001
F	0.015	00010
G	0.011	00011

In a serial stream of 0s and 1s, each character is assigned 8 bits and one character can be separated from another by breaking off 8 bit chunks

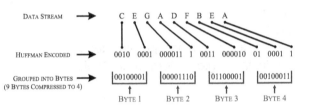

DATA STREAM ➡ C E G A D F B E A

HUFFMAN ENCODED ➡ 0010 0001 000011 1 0011 000010 01 0001 1

GROUPED INTO BYTES ➡ |00100001| |00001110| |01100001| |00100011|
(9 BYTES COMPRESSED TO 4)   ↑   ↑   ↑   ↑
                                  BYTE 1   BYTE 2   BYTE 3   BYTE 4

DB2 uses sequences of characters, according to probability of occurrence, so that fewer bits can be used to achieve compression

A Binary Tree Of Nodes

Huffman encoding compression works by creating a binary tree of nodes. (A node can be either a *leaf node* or an *internal node*.) Initially, all nodes are leaf nodes, which contain the symbol itself, the weight of the symbol (based on frequency of appearance), and optionally, a link to a parent node which makes it easy to read the code (in reverse) starting from any leaf node in the tree.

As a common convention, bit '**0**' represents following the left child and bit '**1**' represents following the right child.

Traversing A Huffman Encoded Binary Node Tree

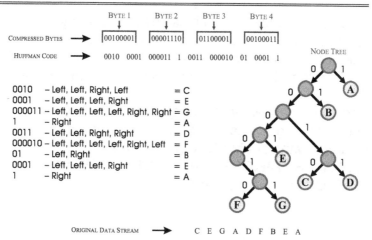

	BYTE 1	BYTE 2	BYTE 3	BYTE 4
COMPRESSED BYTES →	00100001	00001110	01100001	00100011

HUFFMAN CODE → 0010 0001 000011 1 0011 000010 01 0001 1

NODE TREE

Code	Path	Letter
0010	– Left, Left, Right, Left	= C
0001	– Left, Left, Left, Right	= E
000011	– Left, Left, Left, Left, Right, Right	= G
1	– Right	= A
0011	– Left, Left, Right, Right	= D
000010	– Left, Left, Left, Left, Right, Left	= F
01	– Left, Right	= B
0001	– Left, Left, Left, Right	= E
1	– Right	= A

ORIGINAL DATA STREAM → C E G A D F B E A

Data Remains Compressed During Evaluation

Another benefit of actionable compression is that data does not have to be decoded/uncompressed until the DB2 engine is ready to return a result.

During evaluation, predicates (**=**, **<**, **>**, **>=**, **<=**, **BETWEEN**, etc.), joins, and aggregations can be applied directly to encoded values. This results in better query performance since more compressed data can be stored and processed in memory.

A Word About Value Compression

Value compression optimizes space usage by removing duplicate entries for a value, and only storing one copy of the data – the stored copy keeps track of the location of all other references to the data value.

Additionally, when value compression is used, NULLs and zero-length data that has been assigned to columns with variable-length data types (i.e., **VARCHAR, VARGRAPHIC, BLOB, CLOB**, and **DBCLOB**) are not stored on disk.

A Word About Backup Compression

While the use of row and actionable compression can result in smaller backup images, greater storage savings can be realized through the use of backup compression. Row and actionable compression work on a table-by-table basis; with backup compression, *all* of the data in the backup image, including system catalog tables, index objects, LOB objects, and database metadata, is compressed.

Backup compression is performed by executing a **BACKUP DATABASE** command with the **COMPRESS** option specified.

Backup Compression Considerations

Backup compression and row compression can be used together to minimize backup image sizes. However, the use of backup compression requires additional CPU resources and can lengthen the time it takes to perform a backup operation.

Table compression alone can significantly reduce backup storage space requirements; therefore, if row compression is utilized, consider using backup compression only if a reduction in backup storage space is more important than shorter backup times.

4

Monitoring DB2 Activity

Seventeen percent (17%) of the DB2 10.5 Database Administration for LUW Upgrade Exam (Exam 311) is designed to test your ability to monitor a DB2 server environment using the new monitoring tools that are available with DB2 10.5.

The Database System Monitor

Prior to DB2 Version 9.7, database monitoring was performed using a built-in utility known as the *Database System Monitor*, which consisted of two distinct tools:

* ❖ A snapshot monitor that allowed you to capture a "picture" of the state a database environment was in *at a specific point in time.*
* ❖ One or more event monitors that enabled you to capture and log historical information *as specific types of database events took place.*

The In-Memory Metrics Monitoring Infrastructure

In DB2 Version 9.7, a new lightweight monitoring tool called the *In-Memory Metrics Monitoring Infrastructure* was made available (in addition to the Database System Monitor). And, a set of specially designed **monitoring table functions*** and **monitoring views*** were included as part of this infrastructure, allowing DBAs to use the rich query and aggregation of SQL to retrieve and format the monitoring data being collected.

*Additional monitoring table functions and monitoring views have been added with each new release of DB2 since Version 9.7.

Monitoring Table Functions and Views

Monitoring table functions are stored in the **SYSPROC** schema and their names are prefixed with the letters "**MON_GET**"; monitoring views reside in the **SYSIBMADM** schema and their names begin with the letters "**MON**."

The types of data that can be obtained by querying the monitoring table functions and/or views include:

❖ System

Information about server operations associated with processing application requests.

Monitoring Table Functions and Views (Continued)

❖ Activity

Information about the work done to execute the section (access plan) for an SQL statement.

❖ Data objects

Information about operations performed on data objects.

❖ Locking

Information about locks acquired.

❖ System memory

Information about memory usage.

❖ FCM and extent movement

Information related to the fast communications manager (FCM), and about the status of table space extent movement.

Monitor Elements

DB2's monitoring tools store information that is collected in entities called *monitor elements*; the following types of monitor elements are available:

❖ Counter

Keeps a count of the number of times an activity or event has taken place. For example, the **ROWS_READ** *monitor element records the total number of rows that have been read.*

❖ Gauge

Indicates the current value for a particular item. (Gauges can go up or down, depending upon database activity.) For example, the **LOCKS_HELD** *monitor element keeps track of the number of locks that are currently being held.*

Monitor Elements (Continued)

❖ Watermark

Indicates the highest (maximum) or lowest (minimum) value an element has seen since monitoring began. For example, the **UOW_TOTAL_TIME_TOP** *monitor element shows how much time it took for the longest-running transaction to complete.*

❖ Text

Provides reference-type details for a particular monitoring activity or event. For example, the **STMT_TEXT** *monitor element contains the text of an SQL statement that is being executed.*

❖ Timestamp

Indicates the date and time an activity or event took place. For example, the **DB_CONN_TIME** *monitor element shows the date and time the first connection to a database was established (or the date and time a database was activated).*

Monitor Elements Can Often Be Accessed In A Variety Of Ways

Often, the value of a single monitor element can be obtained by querying a variety of monitoring table functions and/or views. For example, the value assigned to the **DB_WORK_CLASS_ID** monitor element can be obtained by querying any of the following monitoring table functions:

❖ `MON_GET_ACTIVITY()`
❖ `MON_GET_ACTIVITY_DETAILS()`
❖ `WLM_GET_WORKLOAD_OCCURRENCE_ACTIVITIES()`

Monitoring Enhancements Added To DB2 Version 10.5

DB2 10.5 contains several enhancements that make monitoring DB2 database environments more comprehensive. These enhancements include:

❖ Monitor elements to measure column data size
❖ Monitor elements to assess buffer pool efficiency
❖ Monitor elements to measure prefetch requests for data in column-organized tables
❖ Monitor elements to measure time spent working with column-organized tables
❖ Monitor elements for the hashed **GROUP BY** operator

New Column Data Size Monitor Elements

The following new monitor elements can be used to estimate the size of column-organized data:

❖ **COL_OBJECT_L_SIZE**

The amount of disk space logically allocated for the data in a particular column-organized table, reported in kilobytes.

❖ **COL_OBJECT_P_SIZE**

The amount of disk space physically allocated for the data in a particular column-organized table, reported in kilobytes.

❖ **COL_OBJECT_L_PAGES**

The number of logical pages used on disk by the data for a particular column-organized table.

New Monitor Elements To Assess Buffer Pool Efficiency

The following new monitor elements aid in the monitoring of data page I/O for column-organized tables:

❖ **POOL_COL_L_READS**

The number of column-organized pages requested from the buffer pool (logical) for regular and large table spaces.

❖ **POOL_COL_P_READS**

The number of column-organized pages read in from table space containers (physical) for regular and large table spaces.

❖ **POOL_COL_LBP_PAGES_FOUND**

The number of times that a column-organized page was present in the local buffer pool.

New Monitor Elements To Assess Buffer Pool Efficiency (Continued)

❖ **POOL_COL_WRITES**

The number of times a column-organized page was physically written from buffer pool to disk.

❖ **POOL_ASYNC_COL_READS**

The number of column-organized pages read in from table space containers (physical) by a prefetcher (for regular and large table spaces).

❖ **POOL_ASYNC_COL_READ_REQS**

The number of asynchronous column-organized read requests made by the prefetcher to the operating system.

❖ **POOL_ASYNC_COL_WRITES**

The number of times a buffer pool data page was physically written to disk by either an asynchronous page cleaner or a prefetcher.

New Monitor Elements To Assess Buffer Pool Efficiency (Continued)

❖ **POOL_ASYNC_COL_LBP_PAGES_FOUND**

The number of times a data page was present in a local buffer pool when a prefetcher attempted to access it.

❖ **OBJECT_COL_L_READS**

The number of column-organized pages that were logically read from a buffer pool for a table.

❖ **OBJECT_COL_P_READS**

The number of column-organized pages that were physically read for a table.

❖ **OBJECT_COL_LBP_PAGES_FOUND**

The number of times that a column-organized page for a table was present in a local buffer pool (LBP).

New Prefetch Request Monitor Elements

The following new monitor elements can be used to track the volume of prefetch requests that are made for data in column-organized tables, as well as the number of pages that prefetchers were able to skip because the pages needed were already in memory:

❖ **POOL_QUEUED_ASYNC_COL_REQS**

The number of column-organized prefetch requests successfully added to the prefetch queue.

❖ **POOL_QUEUED_ASYNC_COL_PAGES**

The number of column-organized pages successfully requested for prefetching.

New Prefetch Request Monitor Elements (Continued)

❖ **POOL_FAILED_ASYNC_COL_REQS**

The number of times an attempt to queue a column-organized prefetch request was made but failed.

❖ **SKIPPED_PREFETCH_COL_P_READS**

The number of column-organized pages that an I/O server (prefetcher) skipped because they were already loaded into a buffer pool.

❖ **SKIPPED_PREFETCH_UOW_COL_P_READS**

The number of column-organized pages that an I/O server (prefetcher) skipped because they were already loaded into a buffer pool <u>by an agent in the same unit of work (transaction)</u>.

New Time Spent Monitor Elements

The following new monitor elements can be used to provide information about how DB2 spent time working with column-organized tables:

❖ **TOTAL_COL_TIME**

The time spent accessing columnar data in a query that accesses column-organized tables.

❖ **TOTAL_COL_PROC_TIME**

The time spent processing columnar data in a query that accesses column-organized tables.

❖ **TOTAL_COL_EXECUTIONS**

The total number of times that data in column-organized tables was accessed.

New Hashed GROUP BY Operator Monitor Elements

The following new monitor elements can be used to analyze sort memory consumption during hashed **GROUP BY** operations*:

❖ **TOTAL_HASH_GRPBYS**

The total number of hashed **GROUP BY** *operations.*

❖ **ACTIVE_HASH_GRPBYS**

The number of **GROUP BY** *operations using hashing as their grouping method that are currently running and consuming sort heap memory.*

****GROUP BY** *operations on column-organized tables use hashing as the grouping method.*

New Hashed GROUP BY Operator Monitor Elements (Continued)

❖ HASH_GRPBY_OVERFLOWS

The number of times that **GROUP BY** *operations using hashing as their grouping method exceeded the sort heap memory available.*

❖ POST_THRESHOLD_HASH_GRPBYS

The total number of hashed **GROUP BY** *sort memory requests that were limited because of a concurrent use of the shared or private sort heap space.*

❖ ACTIVE_HASH_GRPBYS_TOP

The high watermark for the number of hash **GROUP BY** *operations that were active at any one time.*

Functions That Query The New Monitor Elements

Several monitor table functions can be used to obtain values that have been assigned to the new monitor elements that were introduced in DB2 10.5. These functions include:

❖ MON_GET_DATABASE()

Returns database level information within the monitor infrastructure.

❖ MON_GET_DATABASE_DETAILS()

Retrieves database metrics and returns the information in an XML document.

❖ MON_GET_CONNECTION()

Returns metrics for one or more connections.

Functions That Query The New Monitor Elements (Continued)

❖ **MON_GET_CONNECTION_DETAILS ( )**

Retrieves metrics for one or more connections and returns the information in an XML document.

❖ **MON_GET_BUFFERPOOL ( )**

Returns monitor metrics for one or more buffer pools.

❖ **MON_GET_TABLESPACE ( )**

Returns monitor metrics for one or more table spaces.

❖ **MON_GET_TABLE ( )**

Returns metrics for one or more tables.

❖ **MON_GET_TABLE_USAGE_LIST ( )**

Returns information from a usage list that has been defined for a table.

Functions That Query The New Monitor Elements (Continued)

❖ **MON_GET_WORKLOAD ( )**

Returns metrics for one or more workloads.

❖ **MON_GET_WORKLOAD_DETAILS ( )**

Retrieves metrics for one or more workloads and returns the information in an XML document.

❖ **MON_GET_UNIT_OF_WORK ( )**

Returns metrics for one or more transactions (units of work).

❖ **MON_GET_UNIT_OF_WORK_DETAILS ( )**

Retrieves metrics for one or more transactions and returns the information in an XML document.

Functions That Query The New Monitor Elements (Continued)

❖ **MON_GET_SERVICE_SUBCLASS()**

Returns metrics for one or more service subclasses.

❖ **MON_GET_SERVICE_SUBCLASS_DETAILS()**

Retrieves metrics for one or more service subclasses and returns the information in an XML document.

❖ **MON_GET_ACTIVITY()**

Returns a list of all activities that were submitted by the specified application that have not yet been completed.

❖ **MON_GET_ACTIVITY_DETAILS()**

Retrieves metrics about an activity, including general activity information and a set of metrics for the activity, and returns the data collected in an XML document.

Functions That Query The New Monitor Elements (Continued)

❖ **MON_GET_PKG_CACHE_STMT()**

Returns a point-in-time view of both static and dynamic SQL statements in the database package cache (which can reveal how many rows have been written to or read from a column-organized table).

❖ **MON_GET_PKG_CACHE_STMT_DETAILS()**

Retrieves metrics for one or more package cache entries and returns the information in an XML document.

❖ **EVMON_FORMAT_UE_TO_XML()**

Extracts binary events from an unformatted event table and formats them into an XML document.

❖ **MON_FORMAT_XML_METRICS_BY_ROW()**

Returns formatted, row-based output for all metrics contained in an XML metrics document.

The Explain Facility

The Explain Facility allows you to capture and view detailed information about the access plan that was chosen for a particular SQL statement. This information includes performance data (measured in *timerons*) that can be used to identify poorly written queries or flaws in a database's design.

In DB2 10.5, Explain information can also be used to determine how an application performs when it works with column-organized data.

Changes To The Explain Tables

The Explain facility uses a special set of tables to capture access plan information; in DB2 10.5, the following changes were made to the Explain tables to support column-organized tables/data:

❖ EXPLAIN_ARGUMENT

When the **ARGUMENT_TYPE** *column of this table contains the value* **"TQORIGIN,"** *the* **ARGUMENT_VALUE** *column of this table can contain the value* **"COLUMN-ORGANIZED DATA."** *This combination of values is used to indicate that a Columnar Table Queue (CTQ) operator is being used to transfer data from column-organized processing to row-organized processing.*

Changes To The Explain Tables (Continued)

❖ EXPLAIN_OBJECT

*The **OBJECT_TYPE** column of this table can contain the value "**CO**," which is a 2-character descriptive label that indicates the record is for a column-organized table.*

❖ OBJECT_METRICS

The following columns were added to this table:

- OBJECT_COL_L_READS
- OBJECT_COL_P_READS
- OBJECT_COL_GBP_L_READS
- OBJECT_COL_GBP_P_READS
- OBJECT_COL_GBP_INVALID_PAGES
- OBJECT_COL_LBP_PAGES_FOUND
- OBJECT_COL_GBP_INDEP_PAGES_FOUND_IN_LBP

Ways To Collect Explain Data

Explain data can be captured by:

- ❖ Executing the **EXPLAIN** statement
- ❖ Setting the **CURRENT EXPLAIN MODE** special register
- ❖ Setting the **CURRENT EXPLAIN SNAPSHOT** special register
- ❖ Using the **EXPLAIN** option when precompiling or binding an Embedded SQL application
- ❖ Using the **EXPLSNAP** when precompiling or binding an Embedded SQL application

Ways To View Explain Data

Once captured, Explain data can be viewed with the following tools:

- ❖ The **db2expln** command
- ❖ The **dynexpln** command
- ❖ The **db2exfmt** command
- ❖ Visual Explain

Visual Explain is a GUI-based tool; the other tools produce a text-based report that can be displayed on a computer screen or written to an ASCII-formatted file.

Explain Output

Explain output consists of a hierarchical graph that represents the components needed to process the access plan that has been chosen for a particular SQL statement. Each component is represented as a graphical object known as a *node*; two types of nodes can exist:

- ❖ Operator nodes

  Indicates how data is accessed, how tables are joined, and other factors such as whether or not indexes are used.

- ❖ Operand nodes

  Identifies an entity (table, index, or table queue) upon which an operation is performed.

The Columnar Table Queue (CTQ) Operator

New to DB2 10.5, the Columnar Table Queue (**CTQ**) operator is used to represent the transition between column-organized data processing and row-organized data processing.

Ideally, there is only one **CTQ** operator in an access plan and that operator is located near the top of the plan*. (This indicates that almost all of the processing was done using BLU Acceleration.)

*If you see multiple CTQ operators near the bottom of an access plan, you might want to rethink how you are using column-organized tables.

The Columnar Table Queue (CTQ) Operator – Illustrated

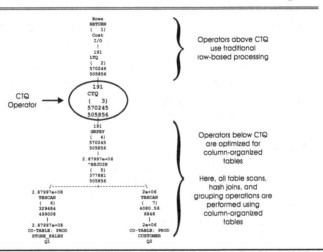

The DB2 Problem Determination Tool (db2pd)

The DB2 Problem Determination Tool is another tool that can be used to gather information about a DB2 environment. Unlike other monitors, this tool attaches directly to DB2 shared memory sets to collect monitor and system information*. And, because it works directly with memory, it can retrieve data quickly in a non-intrusive manner.

The DB2 Problem Determination Tool is invoked by executing the **db2pd** command.

If data is in the process of being changed at the time it is collected, the information retrieved may not be completely accurate.

Improvements To HADR Monitoring

With DB2 10.5, the DB2 Problem Determination Tool can be used to monitor an HADR environment; the **-hadr** option is used with the **db2pd** command to indicate that HADR information is to be collected.

It is important to note that the information returned is dependent upon where the **db2pd** command is executed: if it's executed from a standby server, only information about the primary server and that particular standby is returned; if it's issued from the primary server, information about the primary and all of the standbys available is returned.

Improvements To HADR Monitoring (Continued)

To assist in HADR monitoring, two new columns have also been added to the result table the **MON_GET_HADR()** monitor table function returns:

❖ **HADR_FLAGS**

A space-delimited string containing one or more flags that describe the current state of the HADR environment.

❖ **STANDBY_SPOOL_PERCENT**

Percentage of spool space used, relative to the configured spool limit. When the spool percentage reaches 100%, the standby database will stop receiving logs until space is released as replay proceeds. Spooling can stop before the limit is reached if the standby log path becomes full.

5

High Availability

Seventeen percent (17%) of the DB2
10.5 Database Administration for LUW
Upgrade Exam (Exam 311) is designed
to evaluate your knowledge of the high
availability enhancements that were
introduced in DB2 10.5.

DB2 pureScale

The DB2 pureScale Feature provides scalable, active-active services for database environments; by design, a DB2 pureScale database will continue to process incoming requests, even if multiple components fail simultaneously.

DB2 pureScale Overview

The DB2 pureScale Feature:

❖ **Utilizes a "shared data" architecture**

- *The DB2 engine runs on multiple servers (called members)*
- *Each member has its own buffer pools and log files (which are accessible to other members)*
- *Each member has equal, shared access to the database*

❖ **Provides integrated cluster services**

- *HACMP's Reliable Services Clustering Technology (RCST) quickly detects failures*
- *Tivoli System Automation for Multi-Platforms (SA MP) automates recovery*
- *IBM's General Parallel File System (GPFS) handles shared storage access*

DB2 pureScale Overview (Continued)

❖ Offers application transparency

- *Clients see a single, common view of the database*
- *Clients can connect to any member*
- *Automatic load balancing and client reroute (based on workload) can alter the physical connection being used without the client being aware*

❖ Leverages IBM's System z Sysplex technology

- *Cluster Caching Facility (CF) software provides global locking and buffer pool management*
- *CF serves as the center of communication and coordination between members*
- *Synchronous duplexing of the CF ensures high availability*

DB2 pureScale Overview (Continued)

❖ Utilizes a low-latency, high-speed interconnect to maximize performance

- *Special optimizations provide significant advantages on RDMA-capable interconnects like InfiniBand and 10Gb RoCE Ethernet*
- *No interrupt or other message processing is required*

DB2 pureScale – Illustrated

DB2 10.5 pureScale Feature Enhancements

Several DB2 pureScale enhancements were introduced in DB2 10.5, including:

- ❖ Online topology changes
- ❖ Online fix pack updates
- ❖ Reorganization enhancements
- ❖ Random ordering for index key columns
- ❖ Workload balancing with member subsets (multi-tenancy)
- ❖ Mobility of backup images
- ❖ HADR support

Online Topology Changes

With DB2 10.5, new members can be added to a DB2 pureScale instance while the instance remains online and accessible.

As before, new members are added to a DB2 pureScale cluster by executing the **db2iupdt** command. However, in DB2 10.5, cataloged databases are available on the new member* immediately upon the successful completion of this command.

*The addition of new members no longer requires an offline database backup to be taken before cataloged databases are marked "usable."

Online Fix Pack Updates

Starting with DB2 10.5, it is possible to apply fix pack updates to a DB2 pureScale environment *while the DB2 instance remains available**; this is done by applying the update to one database server at a time while the remaining database servers continue to process transactions. (Immediately after a database server has been updated, it can resume transaction processing.)

*To apply a fix pack in previous releases, the DB2 pureScale instance had to be taken offline. Applying a fix pack offline is still supported, even though it's no longer required.

Reorganization Enhancements

In DB2 10.5, the following reorganization capabilities were made available for DB2 pureScale environments:

* ❖ In-place (online) table reorganization for tables that use adaptive compression.
* ❖ Extent reclamation operations for insert time clustering (ITC) tables (to consolidate sparsely allocated blocks into a smaller number of blocks).

Random Ordering For Index Key Columns

The random ordering of index key columns helps to alleviate page contention on frequently accessed pages in certain **INSERT** scenarios.

If rows are added to a table in the order of an index, the last leaf page of the index is accessed frequently since every key added gets inserted into that page.

When values are stored at random places in the index tree, the number of consecutive insertions on a page decreases. This alleviates page contention, particularly in DB2 pureScale environments where pages are shared between members.

Creating Indexes That Use Random Ordering For Key Columns

To create an index that uses random ordering for index key storage, supply the **RANDOM** clause with the key column definition that is specified in a **CREATE INDEX** statement:

```
CREATE INDEX dept_idx
  ON department(dept_id RANDOM)
```

Creates an index named DEPT_IDX that uses random ordering to store its key column values

Key column values that are stored in random order can be used in non-matching index scans; index-only access on random key columns is also possible.

Workload Balancing With Member Subsets (Multi-Tenancy)

Previously, an application could either be configured to run on a single member of a DB2 pureScale cluster (*client affinity*) or across all of the cluster members (*workload balancing*) – there were no other options.

Beginning with DB2 10.5, FixPack 1, it is possible to isolate application workloads to one or more specific members that have been assigned to a *member subset*. By using member subsets, batch processing can be isolated from transactional workloads and multiple databases within a single instance can be separated from one another.

Mobility Of Backup Images

With DB2 10.5, it's possible to restore an offline database backup image that was taken on a DB2 Enterprise Server Edition instance to a DB2 pureScale instance (and vice versa). It's also possible to:

❖ Restore a database backup image taken on one DB2 pureScale instance to another DB2 pureScale instance that has a different topology. *(A common member must be present in both the source and target DB2 pureScale instances.)*
❖ Restore table space backup images taken on one DB2 pureScale instance to a DB2 pureScale instance with a superset topology.

High Availability Disaster Recovery (HADR)

HADR protects against data loss by replicating data changes from a source database, called the *primary*, to one or more (up to three) target databases, called *standbys*. (When HADR is deployed in multiple standby mode, one target is designated as the *principal HADR standby database* and any additional standbys used are referred to as *auxiliary HADR standby databases*.)

The roles of the primary and a standby database can be switched by executing the **TAKEOVER HADR <BY FORCE>** command.

Setting Up An HADR Environment

To set up an HADR environment, perform the following steps (in the order shown):

1. Back up the database on the primary server.
2. Restore the database on the standby server(s).
3. Obtain the host name, host IP address, and service name (or port number) for each server.
4. Decide on a synchronization mode to use.
5. Update the HADR-specific database configuration parameters on each server.
6. Start HADR on the standby server(s).
7. Start HADR on the primary server.

HADR Synchronization Modes

The HADR synchronization mode used determines the degree of protection against data loss provided. Four synchronization modes are available:

❖ Synchronous (**SYNC**)

Longest transaction response time; greatest protection against data loss. (Writes are considered successful only when log records have been written to log files on the standby server.)

❖ Near synchronous (**NEARSYNC**)

Slightly shorter response time than synchronous mode; slightly less protection against data loss. (Writes are considered successful only when log records have been written to main memory on the standby server.)

HADR Synchronization Modes (Continued)

❖ Asynchronous (**ASYNC**)

Slightly shorter response time than near synchronous mode; slightly less protection against data loss. (Writes are considered successful only when log records have been written to the TCP layer of the primary server.)

❖ Super asynchronous (**SUPERASYNC**)

Shortest transaction response time; highest probability of data loss. (Writes are considered successful only when log records have been written to log files on the primary server.)

DB2 pureScale and HADR Support

Starting with DB2 10.5, HADR can be used to provide disaster recovery protection to DB2 pureScale environments.

Configuring and managing HADR in a DB2 pureScale environment is very similar to configuring and managing HADR in a traditional DB2 environment. However, only the **db2pd** command and the MON_GET_HADR() table function can be used for HADR monitoring; other monitoring interfaces do not report HADR information when used with DB2 pureScale.

HADR Restrictions In DB2 pureScale Environments

The following restrictions apply when HADR is used in a DB2 pureScale environment:

* ❖ The synchronous (**SYNC**) and near synchronous (**NEARSYNC**) synchronization modes are not supported; only asynchronous (**ASYNC**) and super asynchronous (**SUPERASYNC**) can be used.
* ❖ Only one HADR standby database is allowed; multiple standbys are not supported.
* ❖ "Peer windows" do not exist.
* ❖ The "reads on standby" feature is not supported.
* ❖ Network address translation (NAT) between primary and standby sites is not supported.

HADR Restrictions In DB2 pureScale Environments (Continued)

* ❖ The primary and standby clusters must have the same member topology; that is, *each instance must have the same number of DB2 members and each member must have the same member ID*.
* ❖ The primary and standby clusters must have the same number of cluster caching facilities (CFs).
* ❖ IBM's Tivoli System Automation for Multi-Platforms (SA MP) cannot be used to manage automatic failover. (SA MP is responsible for managing high availability within the local cluster only.)

HADR Standby Replay In DB2 pureScale Environments

In a DB2 pureScale-HADR environment, only one member of the standby cluster replays logs – all other members remain inactive. Members in the primary cluster ship their logs to the replay member at the standby using a TCP connection; the replay member merges and replays the log streams.

If the standby cannot connect to a particular member on the primary, another member on the primary (that the standby can connect to) sends the logs for the unconnected member. This is known as *assisted remote catchup*.

HADR Takeover Operations With DB2 pureScale

With HADR, two types of takeover operations can be performed. They are:

❖ Role switch

> *Swaps the role of the primary and the standby. Role switch is initiated by executing the* **TAKEOVER HADR** *command (from any member of the standby cluster) and can only be performed when the primary is available.*

❖ Failover

> *Makes the standby the new primary and sends a message to the old primary to disable it. Failover is initiated by executing the* **TAKEOVER HADR BY FORCE** *command (from any member of the standby cluster) and can only be performed when the primary is unavailable.*

HADR Takeover Operations With DB2 pureScale (Continued)

When either takeover operation is performed in a DB2 pureScale environment, after the standby completes the transition to the primary role, the database is only started on the DB2 member that served as the replay member before the takeover occurred.

To start the database on the other members, the **ACTIVATE DATABASE** command must be executed *or* a connection to the database must be established.

DB2 Advanced Copy Services (ACS)

DB2 Advanced Copy Services (ACS) allows the fast copying technology of a storage device to be used to perform the data copying task of backup and restore operations. (A backup image that is created with DB2 ACS is known as a "snapshot" backup.)

In previous versions of DB2, a DB2 ACS API driver for the storage device being used had to exist before snapshot backup and restore operations could be performed.

The DB2 ACS Script Interface

With DB2 10.5, if you want to perform snapshot operations on a storage device that doesn't have a vendor-supplied DB2 ACS API driver, you can do so by creating a DB2 ACS script. Such a script allows the DB2 ACS library (which is included with DB2) to communicate directly with a storage subsystem to back up and restore volumes that contain database data and transaction logs.

DB2 ACS scripts are utilized by providing the name of the script and the **SCRIPT** clause or **-script** parameter with the appropriate DB2 command or API.

DB2 ACS Script Types

Three types of DB2 ACS scripts can exist:

❖ Snapshot backup

   Performs the actions needed to create a snapshot backup image.

❖ Snapshot restore

   Performs the actions needed to restore a database from a snapshot backup image.

❖ Snapshot management

   Performs the actions needed to delete a snapshot backup image.

DB2 ACS Snapshot Backup Script Actions

A snapshot backup script can execute the following actions:

❖ **prepare**

Runs any actions that need to take place before the snapshot backup operation is performed.

❖ **snapshot**

Performs the snapshot backup operation.

❖ **verify**

Verifies that a snapshot backup image was successfully produced.

DB2 ACS Snapshot Backup Script Actions (Continued)

❖ **rollback**

Cleans up the backup image if the snapshot operation fails.

❖ **store_metadata**

Specifies actions that can occur after a snapshot backup image has been produced and all required metadata has been written to a protocol file.

DB2 ACS Snapshot Restore Script Actions

A snapshot restore script can execute the following actions:

❖ prepare

Runs any actions that need to take place before the snapshot restore operation is performed.

❖ restore

Performs the snapshot restore operation.

DB2 ACS Snapshot Management Script Actions

A snapshot management script can execute the following actions:

❖ prepare

Runs any actions that need to take place before a snapshot delete operation is performed.

❖ delete

Performs a snapshot delete operation.

DB2 ACS Protocol Files

DB2 ACS scripts work in conjunction with DB2 ACS protocol files. These files, which are created by the DB2 ACS library, contain information that is needed to perform snapshot operations. Essentially, DB2 ACS protocol files serve three purposes:

- ❖ They show the progress of a running operation
- ❖ They supply a script with information and options that are provided by the DB2 ACS library
- ❖ In the event an operation fails, they provide information that can be used for debugging

DB2 ACS Protocol File Sections

A DB2 ACS protocol file is divided into different sections, each of which shows the progress and options of each DB2 ACS API function call. The information in each section consists of the following:

- ❖ The DB2 ACS API function name
- ❖ The beginning and ending timestamp for when the function started and ended
- ❖ Commands that were used to invoke the script
- ❖ Any options that were provided with the function call

DB2 ACS Protocol File Section Example

A DB2 ACS protocol file written for a snapshot backup script might begin with an entry that looks something like this:

```
# ===================================================
# db2ACSInitialize(): BEGIN [2016-01-30 08:15:45]
EXTERNAL_SCRIPT=/home/db2inst1/libacssc.sh
HANDLE=1354281345
START_TIME=1354281345
DB_NAME=SAMPLE
INSTANCE=db2inst1
DBPARTNUM=0
SIGNATURE=SQL10020
EXTERNAL_OPTIONS=/home/db2inst1/repository 2ndoption
# db2ACSInitialize(): END
# ===================================================
```

6

Utilities

Thirteen percent (13%) of the DB2 10.5 Database Administration for LUW Upgrade Exam (Exam 311) is designed to test your knowledge of the new utilities that were introduced with DB2 10.5.

IBM InfoSphere Optim Tools

The IBM InfoSphere Optim product family of data lifecycle management tools offer a way to design, develop, deploy, and manage database environments and applications. This product family consists of:

❖ **IBM InfoSphere Data Architect**

Provides a collaborative data design solution that enables you to discover, model, visualize, relate, standardize, and integrate diverse and distributed data assets.

❖ **IBM InfoSphere Optim Configuration Manager**

Offers centralized configuration management of client applications and databases.

IBM InfoSphere Optim Tools (Continued)

❖ **IBM InfoSphere Optim High Performance Unload**

Offers a high-speed solution for unloading, extracting, and repartitioning data.

❖ **IBM InfoSphere Optim Performance Manager**

Provides information that can help identify, diagnose, solve, and pro-actively prevent performance problems.

❖ **IBM InfoSphere Optim pureQuery Runtime**

Provides a runtime environment and application programming interface (API) that enhances the performance, security, and manageability of database client applications.

❖ **IBM InfoSphere Optim Query Tuner**

Offers expert advice on writing high-quality queries and improving database design.

IBM InfoSphere Optim Tools (Continued)

❖ IBM InfoSphere Optim Query Workload Tuner

*Provides expert recommendations to help improve the performance of SQL queries and query workloads. **(With the full licensed version, this tool will also generate the DDL needed to create or modify indexes that can improve performance.)***

❖ IBM InfoSphere Optim Query Tuner Workflow Assistant

*A Data Studio GUI interface for IBM InfoSphere Optim Query Workload Tuner that can be used to format an SQL query such that each table reference, each column reference, and each predicate is presented on its own line, which can be expanded to drill down into the parts of a query so its structure can be better understood. **(Before the Optim Query Tuner Workflow Assistant will collect new Explain information for the same SQL statement, the catalog cache must be updated.)***

The Optim Workload Table Organization Advisor

Introduced with DB2 10.5, the **Optim Workload Table Organization Advisor** (OWTOA) examines all tables that are referenced by SQL statements in a workload and makes recommendations on which row-organized tables to convert to column-organized tables.

This is the only tool that can make this type of recommendation.

OWTOA's Workload Access Plan Comparison Feature

The **Workload Access Plan Comparison** feature of the Optim Workload Table Organization Advisor can be used to fix or compare data access plans.

Using this tool, the access plans from two Explain snapshots can be compared to validate Query Workload Tuner recommendations. To make such a comparison, Explain data would need to be generated for the original queries, the workload would then need to be tuned, Explain data would then have to be generated for the new queries, and finally, both sets of Explain data would need to be compared.

DB2's Data Movement Utilities

DB2 provides four utilities that can be used to transfer data between DB2 databases and external files; they are:

- ❖ The Export utility
- ❖ The Import utility
- ❖ The Load utility
- ❖ The Ingest utility

The Export Utility

The Export utility is used to retrieve data from a DB2 database and copy it to an external file.

The Export utility can be invoked by executing the **EXPORT** command.

The Import Utility

The Import utility is used to retrieve data from an external file and copy it to a DB2 database.

The Import utility can be invoked by executing the **IMPORT** command.

The Load Utility

Like the Import utility, the Load utility can be used to bulk-load data into a table. However, the way in which each utility moves data between external files and tables is significantly different – the Import utility copies data using insert and update operations while the Load utility (which can be invoked by executing the **LOAD** command) builds pages from the data and writes those pages directly to the appropriate table space container(s)*.

The Load utility cannot be used to populate system tables, temporary tables, or tables that do not already exist.

The LOAD Command

Basic syntax for the **LOAD** command is:

```
LOAD <CLIENT> FROM [ [FileName | PipeName | Device |
   Cursor] ,...] OF [DEL | ASC | IXF]
<LOBS FROM [LOBPath ,... ]> <XML FROM [XMLPath ,... ]>
<MODIFIED BY [Modifier ,... ]> <Method>
<SAVECOUNT [SaveCount]> <MESSAGES [MsgFileName]>
[INSERT | REPLACE <KEEPDICTIONARY |
   RESETDICTIONARY> | RESTART | TERMINATE]
INTO [TableName] <( [ColumnName ,... ] )>
<FOR EXCEPTION [ExTableName]>
<COPY NO | COPY YES TO [Location] | NONRECOVERABLE>
<INDEXING MODE [AUTOSELECT | REBUILD | INCREMENTAL |
   DEFERRED]>
<STATISTICS NO | STATISTICS USE PROFILE>
```

Controlling How LOAD Affects The Target Table

❖ INSERT

Data is appended to the target table (which must already exist).

❖ REPLACE <KEEPDICTIONARY | RESETDICTIONARY>

Existing data is deleted from the target table; new data is added. (A new compression dictionary can be built at this time while an existing compression dictionary can be kept or be recreated.)

❖ RESTART

Any previous Load operation that failed or was terminated will be continued from the last point of consistency established.

❖ TERMINATE

*Load operation is terminated; new data added is either backed out (**INSERT**) or truncated (**REPLACE**).*

Effects Of COPY NO, COPY YES, and NONRECOVERABLE

❖ COPY NO

If the database is recoverable, the table space in which the table resides will be placed in "Backup Pending" state and data in any table stored in that table space cannot be modified until a backup image of the database or table space is created.

❖ COPY YES

If the database is recoverable, a copy of the loaded data will be written to the location specified.

❖ NONRECOVERABLE

The transaction performing the load is marked "unrecoverable" and any subsequent roll-forward recovery operation will mark the table that was loaded as being "Invalid"; the table will then have to be dropped (or restored from a backup image).

Effects Of The INDEXING MODE Clause

❖ AUTOSELECT

The Load utility will automatically decide whether to rebuild or extend indexes.

❖ REBUILD

All indexes will be rebuilt.

❖ INCREMENTAL

Existing indexes will be extended with new data.

❖ DEFERRED

The Load utility will not attempt index creation; instead, indexes will be marked as needing to be refreshed.

Effects Of STATISTICS NO and STATISTICS USE PROFILE

❖ STATISTICS NO

Specifies that statistics are not to be collected. **This is the default behavior for row-organized tables.**

❖ STATISTICS USE PROFILE*

Instructs the Load utility to collect statistics during the load operation, using the statistics profile that has been defined for the table being loaded. (A statistics profile specifies the type of statistics that are to be collected for a particular table; a statistics profile can be created with the **RUNSTATS** *command.)* **This is the default behavior for column-organized tables.**

*A statistics profile should exist before the **STATISTICS USE PROFILE** *option is used; if a profile doesn't exist, statistics will be collected using the default options that are used to perform automatic* **RUNSTATS** *operations.*

LOAD Exception Tables

Exception tables are user-created tables that mirror the definition of tables that are being loaded *or* that are being checked by the **SET INTEGRITY** statement.

In the case of Load operations, exception tables are used to store copies of rows that are encountered (as data is being loaded) that violate unique index rules, range constraints, or security policies.

The LOAD Command – Illustrated

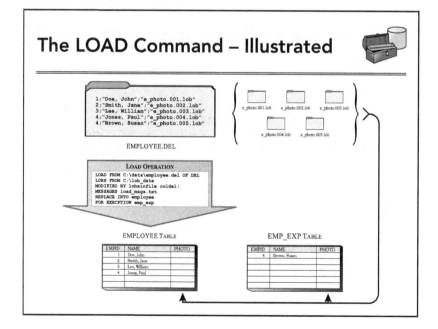

Load Operation Phases

A load operation has several distinct phases; they are, in order:

- ❖ Analyze
- ❖ Load
- ❖ Build
- ❖ Delete
- ❖ Index copy

The **Analyze** phase is *only* used when data is loaded into column-organized tables; the **Index copy** phase is *only* used when row-organized tables are loaded.

What Gets Done During Each Load Phase

- ❖ Analyze

  During the analyze phase, a column compression dictionary is built, if needed (which is the case if a **LOAD REPLACE, LOAD REPLACE RESETDICTIONARY,** *or* **LOAD REPLACE RESETDICTIONARYONLY** *operation is performed; this is also the case if a* **LOAD INSERT** *operation is performed against an empty column-organized table).* ***This phase is not performed if the table being loaded is a row-organized table.***

- ❖ Load

  During the load phase, data is loaded into the table, and index keys and table statistics are collected, if appropriate.

What Gets Done During Each Load Phase (Continued)

❖ Build

During the build phase, indexes are produced based on the index keys collected during the load phase. The indexes produced may be stored in a system temporary table space at this time.

❖ Delete

During the delete phase, rows that violated a unique or primary key are removed from the table. The deleted rows will be written to an exception table if one was specified.

❖ Index copy

During the index copy phase, index data is copied from a system temporary table space to the appropriate table space for permanent storage (if necessary). **This phase is not performed if the table being loaded is a column-organized table.**

The Ingest Utility

The Ingest utility is a high-speed, client-side utility that is used to stream real-time data from files and named pipes into tables stored in a DB2 database. Because it can move large amounts of data without having to acquire table-level locks, the Ingest utility provides the greatest level of data concurrency and availability of all the DB2 data movement utilities available.

The Ingest utility can be invoked by executing the **INGEST** command.

A Word About The ADMIN_MOVE_TABLE() Procedure

The `ADMIN_MOVE_TABLE()` procedure can be used to move data from an active table to a new table that has the same name, *while the data remains online and accessible.*

When this procedure is called with the **MOVE** option specified, the table move process is performed in a single step. To have more control over the process (for example, to manage when the target table is taken offline), this procedure may be called multiple times – once to perform each of the following operations: **INIT**, **COPY**, **REPLAY**, and **SWAP**.

The db2convert Utility

The db2convert utility is used to convert row-organized tables into column-organized tables; this utility is invoked by executing the **db2convert** command.

To ensure that tables being converted remain online and accessible throughout the conversion process, the db2convert utility calls the `ADMIN_MOVE_TABLE()` procedure.

The db2convert Command

Basic syntax for the **db2convert** command is:

```
db2convert -d [DatabaseName]
<-stopBeforeSwap | -continue >
<-z [SchemaName] <-t [TableName]>>
<-ts [TargetTableSpace]>
<-opt [COPY_USE_LOAD | 'AMT_Options']>
<-force>
<-o [OutputFile]>
<-check>
```

db2convert Command Options

❖ -d [*DatabaseName*]

Specifies the name of the database that contains the row-organized user tables that are to be converted.

❖ -stopBeforeSwap

Specifies that the utility is to stop before performing the **SWAP** *phase of the* **ADMIN_MOVE_TABLE()** *procedure and prompt the user to perform an online backup operation before continuing.*

❖ -continue

Specifies that the utility is to perform the **SWAP** *and* **CLEANUP** *phases of the* **ADMIN_MOVE_TABLE()** *procedure to finish the conversion process.*

db2convert Command Options (Continued)

❖ -z [*SchemaName*]

Specifies the schema name of one or more tables to convert.

❖ -t [*TableName*]

Specifies the unqualified name of the table to convert.

❖ -ts [*TargetTableSpace*]

Specifies the table space in which the column-organized table(s) being produced are to be created.

❖ -opt COPY_USE_LOAD

Specifies that the **ADMIN_MOVE_TABLE()** *procedure is to copy the data by default.*

db2convert Command Options (Continued)

❖ -opt '*AMT_Options*'

Specifies one or more options, separated by commas, that are to be passed to the **ADMIN_MOVE_TABLE()** *procedure.*

❖ -force

Specifies that all table types are to be converted, including range-partitioned tables, multidimensional clustering (MDC) tables, and insert time clustering (ITC) tables.

❖ -o [*OutputFile*]

Specifies the output file to which all messages are to be written.

❖ -check

Specifies that conversion notes are to be generated and displayed, but that the actual conversion process is not to take place.

db2convert Examples

db2convert -d hr_data -stopBeforeSwap

Starts the process that will convert all of the user tables found in a database named HR_DATA to column-organized tables, and prompts the user to perform an online backup operation before continuing

db2convert -d hr_data -continue

Continues a process to convert all row-organized user tables found in a database named HR_DATA that was started earlier (and then paused)

db2convert -d test -z db2inst1 -t sales

Converts a row-organized user table named SALES (stored in a schema named DB2INST1 in a database named TEST) into a column-organized table

APPENDIX A

DB2 10.5 DBA for LUW Upgrade from DB2 10.1 Exam (Exam 311) Objectives

The *DB2 10.5 DBA for LUW Upgrade from DB2 10.1* exam (Exam 311) consists of 30 questions, and candidates have 60 minutes to complete the exam. A score of 60 percent or higher is required to pass.

The primary objectives the *IBM DB2 10.5 DBA for LUW Upgrade from DB2 10.1* exam (Exam 311) is designed to cover are as follows:

Server Management (17%)

- Ability to configure a DB2 system for analytics workloads—DB2SET DB2_WORKLOAD=ANALYTICS (DFT_TABLE_ORG = COLUMN, DFT_EXTENT_SZ = 4, DFT_DEGREE = ANY; database page size = 32K)
- Ability to use autonomic features with DB2 10.5 BLU Acceleration—automatic RUNSTATS and automatic space reclamation for column-organized tables
- Knowledge of Data Studio 4.1

- Ability to use automated workload management when DB2_WORKLOAD is set to ANALYTICS

Physical Design (37%)

- Knowledge of the seven "big ideas" behind DB2 10.5 BLU Acceleration:
    1. Simple to implement and use (no indexes, MDC tables, MQTs, partitioning, or statistical views)
    2. Friendly approximate Huffman encoding (actionable compression)
    3. Use of SIMD instruction sets
    4. Maximized use of CPU cache
    5. Columnar data store
    6. Memory caching facility
    7. Data skipping
- Knowledge of and ability to implement compression features (i.e., static compression, adaptive compression, column-organized table compression, value compression, and backup compression)
- Ability to use expression-based indexes, as well as collect statistics on expression-based indexes (RUNSTATS, statistics profiles, automatic statistics collection)
- Ability to create indexes that exclude NULL keys
- Knowledge of Oracle-compatibility features
- Ability to create and use unique and primary key informational constraints
- Knowledge of extended row size support

Monitoring (17%)

- Ability to use new monitor elements to measure column data size

- Ability to use new monitor elements to measure time spent in the Columnar Data Engine (CDE)
- Ability to use new monitor elements to track dynamic prefetch requests for data in column-organized tables
- Knowledge of new Explain enhancements
- Ability to recognize the Columnar Table Queue (CTQ) operator in Explain output, as well as knowledge of what it represents
- Knowledge of the monitoring function MON_GET_ROUTINE()
- Knowledge of HADR monitoring enhancements

High Availability (17%)

- Knowledge of enhancements to DB2 pureScale
- Ability to use online REORG in a DB2 pureScale environment
- Knowledge of how to replay a member in a DB2 pureScale standby cluster
- Ability to set up HADR in a DB2 pureScale environment
- Ability to apply rolling FixPack updates in a DB2 pureScale environment
- Knowledge of multi-tenancy in a DB2 pureScale environment
- Knowledge of explicit hierarchical locking multi-tenancy in a DB2 pureScale environment
- Knowledge of DB2 Advanced Copy Services customized scripts

Utilities (13%)

- Ability to use the IBM Optim Query Workload Tuner
- Knowledge of the Workload Table Organization Advisor (support for comparing access plans before and after)
- Knowledge of the ANALYZE phase for Load operations that are performed against column-organized tables

- Knowledge of default AUTOMATIC STATISTICS COLLECTION behavior when the Load utility is used to populate column-organized tables
- Ability to use the db2convert utility

Practice Questions

Welcome to the section that really makes this book unique. In my opinion, one of the best ways to prepare for the *DB2 10.5 DBA for LUW Upgrade from DB2 10.1* certification exam (Exam 311) is by answering practice questions that are similar to, and that are presented in the same format as, the questions you will see when you take the actual exam. In this part of the book you will find 56 practice questions, as well as comprehensive answers for each question. (It's not enough to know *which* answer is correct; it's also important to know *why* a particular answer is correct—and why the other choices are wrong!)

All the questions presented here were developed using copious notes that were taken during the exam development process. (As a member of the team that developed the *DB2 10.5 DBA for LUW Upgrade from DB2 10.1* certification exam, I had the opportunity to see every question that was created for this exam!) I trust you will find these practice questions helpful.

Roger E. Sanders

DB2 Server Management

Question 1

Which statement about the DB2_WORKLOAD registry variable is NOT TRUE?

O   A.   A value can be assigned to the DB2_WORKLOAD registry variable with the db2set command.

O   B.   Once the value ANALYTICS has been assigned to the DB2_WORKLOAD registry variable, only single-partition databases can be created.

O   C.   The DB2_WORKLOAD registry variable can be used to configure memory, page size and extent size, as well as enable column organization and workload management.

O   D.   When the value ANALYTICS is assigned to the DB2_WORKLOAD registry variable, by default, the value 32 is assigned to the DFT_EXTENT_SZ database parameter for all newly created databases.

Question 2

Which two commands, when executed, will cause all tables that are created in a database named MY_DB to be column-organized, by default? (Choose two.)

☐   A.   db2set DB2_WORKLOAD=ANALYTICS

☐   B.   db2set DB2_COLUMN_ORGANIZED=YES

☐   C.   db2set DB2_BLU_ACCELERATION=ENABLED

☐   D.   UPDATE DB CFG FOR my_db USING DFT_COL_ORG ON

☐   E.   UPDATE DB CFG FOR my_db USING DFT_TABLE_ORG COLUMN

Question 3

In DB2 10.5, which feature is NOT available with the SQL Warehousing Tool (SQW)?

O   A.   SQL pooling

O   B.   BLU Acceleration

O   C.   Secure Shell (SSH) protocol support in the Administration Console

O   D.   Ability to establish a secure connection without a password in Design Studio

Question 4

When the DB2_WORKLOAD registry variable is set to ANALYTICS, which database
configuration parameter is NOT assigned a value that has been calculated specifically
for an analytics workload?

- ○ A. SORTHEAP
- ○ B. PCKCACHESZ
- ○ C. UTIL_HEAP_SZ
- ○ D. SHEAPTHRES_SHR

Question 5

The following command was executed successfully:

```
db2set DB2_WORKLOAD = ANALYTICS
```

Which database configuration parameter will be assigned the value 4?

- ○ A. PAGESIZE
- ○ B. DFT_DEGREE
- ○ C. UTIL_HEAP_SZ
- ○ D. DFT_EXTENT_SZ

Question 6

If the DB2_WORKLOAD registry variable is set to ANALYTICS, what is done to ensure
that empty extents are automatically returned to table space storage for reuse
whenever data is deleted from column-organized tables?

- ○ A. A default space reclamation policy is installed.
- ○ B. The AUTO_REORG database configuration parameter is set to AUTOMATIC.
- ○ C. The AUTO_TBL_MAINT database configuration parameter is set to RECLAIM_
  EXTENTS.
- ○ D. A storage group named IBMBLUSTOGROUP is created and all column-
  organized tables are placed in it.

Question 7

If the DB2_WORKLOAD registry variable is set to ANALYTICS, which event must take place before intrapartition parallelism will be utilized?

- O A. The instance must be stopped and restarted.
- O B. The database must be stopped and restarted.
- O C. Any existing row-organized tables must be dropped and recreated.
- O D. Any existing column-organized tables must be dropped and recreated.

Question 8

Which two statements about the SYSDEFAULTMANAGEDSUBCLASS service subclass are TRUE? (Choose two.)

- ☐ A. It is the service subclass where user connections are managed.
- ☐ B. It is the service subclass that dictates what is to happen when a work of interest is detected.
- ☐ C. It is the service subclass where heavyweight queries against column-organized tables run.
- ☐ D. It is the service subclass that is used to control the number of lightweight queries that are running concurrently.
- ☐ E. It is created automatically, under the SYSDEFAULTUSERCLASS superclass, for all new DB2 10.5 databases.

Question 9

Which two statements correctly describe how DB2 Workload Manager behavior is affected when a new column-organized database is created? (Choose two.)

- ☐ A. The SYSDEFAULTUSERWAS work action set is enabled by default.
- ☐ B. The SYSDEFAULTUSERWAS work action set is disabled by default.
- ☐ C. The SYSMANAGEDQUERIES work class must be enabled before queries can run in the USRDEFAULTMANAGEDSUBCLASS service subclass.
- ☐ D. Queries meeting the criteria specified in the SYSMANAGEDQUERIES work class will run in the SYSDEFAULTMANAGEDSUBCLASS service subclass.
- ☐ E. Queries meeting the criteria specified in the USRMANAGEDQUERIES work class will run in the USRDEFAULTMANAGEDSUBCLASS service subclass.

Question 10

Which component is NOT provided in DB2 Warehouse?

○ A. DB2 Warehouse Client
○ B. DB2 Warehouse Gateway
○ C. DB2 Warehouse Data Server
○ D. DB2 Warehouse Application Server

Physical Design

Question 11

A database is needed for an environment where the majority of workloads are expected to be analytical/OLAP in nature and queries will typically access more than 5 percent of the data and will involve extensive scanning, grouping, and aggregation. What type of tables should be used?

○ A. Shadow tables
○ B. Row-organized tables
○ C. Column-organized tables
○ D. Materialized query tables

Question 12

A database is needed for an environment where the majority of workloads are expected to be transactional in nature. What type of tables should be used?

○ A. Shadow tables
○ B. Row-organized tables
○ C. Column-organized tables
○ D. Materialized query tables

Question 13

Which two characteristics are related to BLU Acceleration? (Choose two.)

☐ A. "Always on" adaptive row compression.
☐ B. Default and referential integrity informational constraints.
☐ C. Enhanced caching strategy that improves buffer pool utilization.
☐ D. Significantly smaller storage footprint for database transaction logs.
☐ E. Multiplied CPU power that uses Single Instruction Multiple Data (SIMD)
       instructions for many operations.

Question 14

When can it be beneficial to use a mixture of row-organized and column-organized
tables, as opposed to just one table type?

○ A. When the majority of database workloads are transactional in nature.
○ B. When the majority of database workloads are analytical/OLAP in nature.
○ C. When the the majority of database workloads include queries that access
       more than 5 percent of the data and perform extensive scanning, grouping,
       and aggregation.
○ D. When the majority of workloads include a combination of analytic query
       processing and very selective data access, typically involving less than 2
       percent of the data.

Question 15

Which statement about column-organized tables is TRUE?

○ A. Column-organized tables can be referenced as either the source or target of
       an index.
○ B. Column-organized tables can be referenced as either the source or target of a
       trigger.
○ C. Column-organized tables can be referenced as either the source or target of a
       view.
○ D. Column-organized tables can be referenced as either the source or target of a
       nickname.

Question 16

Which statement about column-organized tables is NOT TRUE?

- ○ A. Range (table) partitioning for column-organized tables is not supported.
- ○ B. Automatic REORG operations for column-organized tables is not supported.
- ○ C. Column-organized tables can only be created in automatic storage databases.
- ○ D. Column-organized tables cannot be created if the DB2_COMPATIBILITY_ VECTOR registry variable has been set to ORA.

Question 17

What is value compression used for?

- ○ A. To ensure that NULL and zero-length data that has been assigned to VARCHAR columns will not be stored on disk.
- ○ B. To ensure that values that appear more frequently are compressed at a higher level than values that do not appear as often.
- ○ C. To search for repeating patterns in the data and replace those patterns with 12-bit symbols, which are stored in a dictionary.
- ○ D. To eliminate duplicate values found throughout a database, including catalog tables, index objects, LOB objects, and database metadata.

Question 18

Which statement about backup compression is NOT TRUE?

- ○ A. Backup compression can be used with row compression and actionable compression.
- ○ B. Backup compression requires additional CPU resources and can lengthen backup times.
- ○ C. Backup compression is more effective if data and index objects are stored in the same table space.
- ○ D. If row compression is utilized, backup compression should only be used if smaller backup images is more important than shorter backup times.

Question 19

Which statement about row compression is NOT TRUE?

○ A. Before data in a table can be compressed, the table must first be enabled for compression.

○ B. When adaptive compression is used, no table-level compression dictionary exists; only page-level compression dictionaries are used.

○ C. When a table is enabled for adaptive compression, the entire table is enabled, even if it is a partitioned table that consists of multiple data partitions.

○ D. When a database is converted to DB2 10.5, existing compressed tables will have classic row compression enabled; current and future records will be compressed at the table level.

Question 20

Which statement about index compression is NOT TRUE?

○ A. The ALTER INDEX statement is used to enable or disable an index for compression.

○ B. By default, index compression is enabled for compressed tables, and disabled for uncompressed tables.

○ C. When an existing index is enabled for compression, the table the index was created for must be reorganized before the index's data will be compressed.

○ D. Multidimensional clustering (MDC) or insert time clustering (ITC) block indexes, catalog indexes, XML path indexes, and indexes for temporary tables cannot be enabled for compression.

Question 21

Which two statements about expression-based indexes are TRUE? (Choose two.)

☐ A. When defining an expression-based index, key expressions that use a scalar function are allowed.

☐ B. When defining an expression-based index, a key expression that references a sequence is allowed.

☐ C. Expression-based indexes are best suited for queries that contain some type of reference to a user-defined function.

☐ D. The RUNSTATS command's statistics profile facility cannot be used to gather customized statistics for expression-based index keys.

☐ E. When an expression-based index is created with the UNIQUE option specified, uniqueness will be enforced against the values stored in the index.

Question 22

When an expression-based index is created, what object is automatically created by DB2 and associated with the index?

○ A. An alias
○ B. A trigger
○ C. A package
○ D. A synopsis table

Question 23

When statistics for expression-based index keys are collected, where are they stored?

○ A. In the system catalog
○ B. In a hidden synopsis table
○ C. In a user-defined summary table
○ D. In a system-generated statistical view

Question 24

If the following SQL statement is executed:

```
CREATE TABLE employee
    (name      VARCHAR(50),
     salary    DECIMAL(8,2),
     address   VARCHAR(100))
```

Which SQL statement will successfully create an expression-based index named IDX1?

○ A. `CREATE INDEX idx1 ON employee (UPPER (name))`
○ B. `CREATE INDEX idx1 ON employee EXPRESSION (UPPER (name))`
○ C. `CREATE INDEX idx1 ON employee (EXPRESSION UPPER (name))`
○ D. `CREATE EXPRESSION BASED INDEX idx1 ON employee (UPPER (name))`

Question 25

Which statement about informational constraints is NOT TRUE?

○ A. In DB2 10.5, any constraint can be defined as being an informational constraint.
○ B. A `NOT ENFORCED` primary key can be created for both column-organized and row-organized tables.
○ C. Informational constraints are created by appending the keywords `NOT ENFORCED` to the constraint definition.
○ D. Informational constraints are used to provide the DB2 optimizer with information that may help improve query performance.

Question 26

Which statement about extended row size support is NOT TRUE?

- ○ A. To take advantage of extended row size support, a table must have at least one column with a varying-length string data type.
- ○ B. Extended row size support is enabled by assigning the value ENABLE to the EXTENDED_ROW_SZ database configuration parameter.
- ○ C. When a row whose length exceeds the maximum record length allowed is inserted into a table with extended row size support enabled, a varying-length string column in the table is converted to a large object data type so the record will fit.
- ○ D. When a row whose length exceeds the maximum record length allowed is inserted into a table with extended row size support enabled, a subset of the data stored in a varying-length string column is moved out of the row and stored as a large object.

Question 27

If extended row size support is not enabled for a table, how is the maximum length of a record determined?

- ○ A. By the page size of the database.
- ○ B. By the page size of the table space the table is stored in.
- ○ C. By the value assigned to the DB2_DEFAULT_ROW_SIZE registry variable.
- ○ D. By the value assigned to the MAX_ROW_SZ database configuration parameter.

Question 28

What two things will happen when the UNIQUE and EXCLUDE NULL KEYS clauses are specified with a CREATE INDEX statement? (Choose two.)

- ☐ A. The resulting index will require less storage space, but it will not be as efficient.
- ☐ B. The CREATE INDEX statement will fail; these two clauses can not be used together.
- ☐ C. The CREATE INDEX statement will return a warning, and the UNIQUE clause will be ignored.
- ☐ D. Rows where the index key is NULL are ignored when the uniqueness of table data is enforced.
- ☐ E. An index for which entries will not be made when all parts of the index key contain the NULL value will be created.

Monitoring DB2 Activity

Question 29

What does the monitoring element POOL_COL_L_READS track?

- ○ A. The number of times that a column-organized page was present in the local buffer pool.
- ○ B. The number of column-organized pages that were logically read from a buffer pool for a table.
- ○ C. The number of times that a column-organized page for a table was present in a local buffer pool.
- ○ D. The number of column-organized pages requested from a buffer pool for regular and large table spaces.

Question 30

Which monitor element is used to determine the number of column-organized pages an I/O server (prefetcher) skipped because they were already loaded in a buffer pool?

O A. SKIPPED_PREFETCH_COL_L_READS
O B. SKIPPED_PREFETCH_COL_P_READS
O C. SKIPPED_PREFETCH_UOW_COL_L_READS
O D. SKIPPED_PREFETCH_UOW_COL_P_READS

Question 31

What does the monitoring element POOL_ASYNC_COL_READS track?

O A. The number of column-organized pages that are physically read for a table.
O B. The number of column-organized pages read from table space containers by a prefetcher.
O C. The number of column-organized pages read in from table space containers for regular and large table spaces.
O D. The number of asynchronous column-organized read requests made by the prefetcher to the operating system.

Question 32

Which monitor element is used to determine the number of column-organized pages that an I/O server (prefetcher) skipped because they had already been loaded into a buffer pool by an agent in the same unit of work?

O A. SKIPPED_PREFETCH_COL_L_READS
O B. SKIPPED_PREFETCH_COL_P_READS
O C. SKIPPED_PREFETCH_UOW_COL_L_READS
O D. SKIPPED_PREFETCH_UOW_COL_P_READS

Question 33

Which operator is used to represent the transition between column-organized data processing and row-organized data processing in a query access plan?

- ○ A. Row Table Queue
- ○ B. Row Transition Queue
- ○ C. Columnar Table Queue
- ○ D. Columnar Transition Queue

Question 34

Which statement about the EXPLAIN_OBJECT table is TRUE?

- ○ A. The columns OBJECT_COL_L_READS and OBJECT_COL_P_READS were added to this table in DB2 10.5.
- ○ B. The ARGUMENT_TYPE and ARGUMENT_VALUE columns of this table can indicate when a CTQ operator is used.
- ○ C. When the db2exmig command is executed, the EXPLAIN_ACTUALS and EXPLAIN_STREAM tables are combined to produce this table.
- ○ D. This table can be used to determine if a particular column-organized table was referenced in the access plan that was generated to satisfy an SQL query.

Question 35

What is the monitoring table function MON_GET_PKG_CACHE_STMT() used for?

- ○ A. To obtain information from a usage list that has been defined for a table.
- ○ B. To determine how many rows are returned from all tables in response to a particular query.
- ○ C. To generate a list of all activities that were submitted but have not yet been completed.
- ○ D. To determine how many rows are returned from a specific column-organized table for a particular query.

Question 36

What is the monitoring element TOTAL_HASH_GRPBYS used for?

- O A. To identify database workloads that are currently running and consuming sort heap memory.
- O B. To determine the number of times that GROUP BY operations exceeded the amount of sort heap memory available.
- O C. To help tune database workloads that consist of queries that perform GROUP BY operations against column-organized tables.
- O D. To help tune database workloads by reducing the amount time spent processing data for queries that access row- and column-organized tables.

Question 37

Which two monitoring table functions will return the information collected in an XML document?

- ☐ A. MON_GET_TABLE()
- ☐ B. MON_GET_PKG_CACHE_STMT()
- ☐ C. MON_GET_ACTIVITY_DETAILS()
- ☐ D. MON_GET_TABLE_USAGE_LIST()
- ☐ E. MON_GET_UNIT_OF_WORK_DETAILS()

Question 38

Which two items were added in DB2 10.5 to aid in monitoring high-availability disaster recovery (HADR) in DB2 pureScale environments? (Choose two.)

- ☐ A. The -hadr option of the db2pd command
- ☐ B. The EVMON_HADR_PSCALE procedure
- ☐ C. The MON_HADR_UTILIZATION administrative view
- ☐ D. The HADR_FLAGS column of the MON_GET_HADR() table function
- ☐ E. The STANDBY_SPOOL_PERCENT column of the SNAP_GET_HADR() table function

High Availability

Question 39

Which two high-availability disaster recovery (HADR) features are NOT supported in a DB2 10.5 pureScale environment? (Choose two.)

- ☐ A. Role switching
- ☐ B. Read on standby (RoS)
- ☐ C. Assisted remote catchup
- ☐ D. Multiple standby targets
- ☐ E. ASYNC synchronization mode

Question 40

How do you perform a role switch operation in a DB2 pureScale environment that is using high-availability disaster recovery (HADR)?

- ○ A. Execute the TAKEOVER HADR command from a member of the standby cluster.
- ○ B. Execute the TAKEOVER HADR BY FORCE command from a member of the standby cluster.
- ○ C. Execute the TAKEOVER HADR command from the Cluster Caching Facility (CF) of the standby cluster.
- ○ D. Execute the TAKEOVER HADR BY FORCE command from the Cluster Caching Facility (CF) of the standby cluster.

Question 41

Which two statements about implementing high-availability disaster recovery (HADR) with DB2 10.5 pureScale are TRUE? (Choose two.)

☐ A. The primary and standby clusters must have the same number of CPUs.

☐ B. The primary and standby clusters must have the same number of DB2 members.

☐ C. The primary and standby clusters must have the same amount of back-end storage.

☐ D. The primary and standby clusters must have the same amount of memory (RAM).

☐ E. The primary and standby clusters must have the same number of cluster caching facilities (CFs).

Question 42

A database administrator wants to back up a database from one DB2 pureScale instance and restore it to another. Which two statements about this type of operation are TRUE? (Choose two.)

☐ A. The source and target pureScale systems can have a different cluster topology.

☐ B. The source and target pureScale systems must share the same back-end storage.

☐ C. A common member must be present in both the source and target pureScale systems.

☐ D. The source and target pureScale systems can share the same high-speed interconnect network.

☐ E. A common cluster caching facility (CF) must be present in both the source and target pureScale systems.

Question 43

Which statement about making topology changes to DB2 10.5 pureScale environments is NOT TRUE?

O A. New members are added to a DB2 pureScale cluster by executing the db2iupdt command.

O B. New members can be added to a DB2 pureScale cluster while the instance remains online and accessible.

O C. Cataloged databases are available on a new member immediately after the member is added to a DB2 pureScale cluster.

O D. When new members are added to a DB2 pureScale cluster, an offline database backup operation must be performed.

Question 44

Which statement about the random ordering of index key columns is NOT TRUE?

O A. Index key column values that are stored in random order can be used in non-matching index scans.

O B. The CREATE RANDOM INDEX statement is used to create an index that uses random index key ordering.

O C. When values are stored at random places in an index tree, the number of consecutive insertions on a page decreases.

O D. The random ordering of index key columns alleviates page contention on frequently accessed pages when certain insert scenarios are performed, particularly in DB2 pureScale environments.

Question 45

What is one benefit that DB2 pureScale multi-tenancy provides?

- ○ A. It allows an application to run on all members of a DB2 pureScale cluster.
- ○ B. It allows an application to run on one specific member of a DB2 pureScale cluster.
- ○ C. It allows batch processing to be isolated from transaction processing in DB2 pureScale environments.
- ○ D. It allows OTLP workloads to be run together with analytical workloads in a DB2 pureScale environment.

Question 46

Which statement about applying FixPacks to a DB2 10.5 pureScale cluster is TRUE?

- ○ A. FixPacks are applied to a DB2 pureScale cluster by executing the db2iupdt command.
- ○ B. Before a FixPack can be applied to a DB2 pureScale server, the instance must be taken offline.
- ○ C. Immediately after a DB2 pureScale database server has been updated, it can resume transaction processing.
- ○ D. Immediately after a DB2 pureScale database server has been updated, a database backup operation must be performed.

Question 47

Which two actions would be implemented in a DB2 Advanced Copy Services (ACS) script that is used to restore a database from a snapshot backup? (Choose two.)

- ☐ A. verify
- ☐ B. restore
- ☐ C. prepare
- ☐ D. rollback
- ☐ E. store_metadata

Question 48

What information can NOT be found in each individual section of a DB2 Advanced Copy Services (ACS) protocol file?

- ○ A. The DB2 ACS API function name.
- ○ B. Any commands the DB2 ACS script invoked.
- ○ C. Any options that were provided with the DB2 ACS API function call.
- ○ D. The beginning and ending timestamp for when the DB2 ACS API function started and ended.

Utilities

Question 49

Which statement about Optim Query Tuner Workflow Assistant is NOT TRUE?

- ○ A. Optim Query Tuner Workflow Assistant is a Data Studio GUI interface for IBM InfoSphere Optim Query Workload Tuner.
- ○ B. Before Optim Query Tuner Workflow Assistant will collect new Explain information for the same SQL statement, the catalog cache must be updated.
- ○ C. Optim Query Tuner Workflow Assistant comes with an application programming interface (API) that can be used to enhance the performance and manageability of complex queries.
- ○ D. Optim Query Tuner Workflow Assistant can be used to format a query such that each table reference, each column reference, and each predicate, is shown on its own line, which can be expanded to drill down into the parts of a query.

Question 50

A database administrator wants to do the following:

1. Capture Explain information for several queries.
2. Tune the query workload as recommended.
3. Generate Explain information for the tuned queries.
4. View access plan differences between the original and the tuned queries.

What single tool can be used to accomplish this task?

○ A.   IBM InfoSphere Optim Performance Manager
○ B.   IBM InfoSphere Optim Query Workload Tuner
○ C.   IBM InfoSphere Optim Query Tuner Workflow Assistant
○ D.   IBM InfoSphere Optim Workload Table Organization Advisor

Question 51

Which two statements about the IBM InfoSphere Optim Query Workload Tuner are true? (Choose two.)

☐ A.   The IBM InfoSphere Optim Query Workload Tuner provides recommendations to help improve the performance of SQL queries and query workloads.
☐ B.   The IBM InfoSphere Optim Query Workload Tuner provides information that can help identify, diagnose, solve, and proactively prevent performance problems.
☐ C.   The full-featured, licensed version of IBM InfoSphere Optim Query Workload Tuner will generate the DDL needed to create or modify indexes that can improve performance.
☐ D.   The full-featured, licensed version of the IBM InfoSphere Optim Query Workload Tuner will create reports that summarize the statistics the DB2 optimizer uses to generate data access plans.
☐ E.   The IBM InfoSphere Optim Query Workload Tuner provides a collaborative data design solution that enables you to discover, model, standardize, and integrate diverse and distributed queries.

Question 52

When data is loaded into a column-organized table with the LOAD command, which phase of the Load operation is NOT used?

○ A.   Build
○ B.   Delete
○ C.   Analyze
○ D.   Index copy

Question 53

What is the correct order of the phases that are used when data is loaded into a row-organized table?

○ A.   Analyze, Load, Build, Delete
○ B.   Load, Build, Delete, Index copy
○ C.   Load, Build, Delete, Analyze, Index copy
○ D.   Analyze, Load, Build, Delete, Index copy

Question 54

If a LOAD REPLACE operation is used to populate a column-organized table, during which phase is a column compression dictionary built?

○ A.   Analyze
○ B.   Load
○ C.   Build
○ D.   Delete

Question 55

Which statement about the STATISTICS USE PROFILE option of the LOAD command is NOT TRUE?

○ A. This option is disabled, by default, for row-organized tables.
○ B. This option is enabled, by default, for column-organized tables.
○ C. This option must be used if the NONRECOVERABLE option is specified.
○ D. A statistics profile should exist before this option is used; but is not required.

Question 56

Which parameter of the db2convert command is used to temporarily stop the utility and prompt the user to perform an online backup operation before continuing?

○ A. -check
○ B. -stopBeforeSwap
○ C. -pauseForBackup
○ D. -opt COPY_USE_LOAD

APPENDIX

Answers to Practice Questions

DB2 Server Management

Question 1

The correct answer is **D**. When the value ANALYTICS is assigned to the DB2_WORKLOAD registry variable, by default, the value 4 (not 32) is assigned to the DFT_EXTENT_SZ database parameter for all newly created databases. (The PAGESIZE database configuration parameter is set to 32 KB.)

The DB2_WORKLOAD registry variable is used to configure memory, page size, and extent size, as well as enable column organization and workload management for an analytics workload (*Answer C*). The value ANALYTICS is assigned to the DB2_WORKLOAD registry variable by executing a command that looks like this:

```
db2set DB2_WORKLOAD=ANALYTICS
```

(*Answer A*). And once the value ANALYTICS has been assigned to the DB2_WORKLOAD registry variable, only single-partition databases can be created (*Answer B*).

Question 2

The correct answers are **A** and **E**. Column-organized tables can be created by executing the CREATE TABLE statement with the ORGANIZE BY COLUMN clause specified. However; if you want to create column-organized tables without having to specify the ORGANIZE BY COLUMN clause, you can set the default table organization type to column-organized by assigning the value COLUMN to the DFT_TABLE_ORG database configuration parameter. (This can be done by executing the UPDATE DATABASE CONFIGURATION command.)

The value ANALYTICS is assigned to the DB2_WORKLOAD registry variable by executing a command that looks like this:

```
db2set DB2_WORKLOAD=ANALYTICS
```

And, when the value ANALYTICS is assigned to the DB2_WORKLOAD registry variable, the value COLUMN is automatically assigned to the DFT_TABLE_ORG database configuration parameter.)

There is no DB2_COLUMN_ORGANIZED registry variable (*Answer B*), DB2_BLU_ACCELERATION registry variable (*Answer C*), or DFT_COL_ORG database configuration parameter (*Answer D*).

Question 3

The correct answer is **A**. There is no SQL pooling feature with any DB2 10.5 product. However, starting with DB2 10.5, the following features *are* available with the SQL Warehousing Tool (SQW) component of the DB2 Warehouse Client:

- BLU Acceleration support (*Answer B*)
- Oracle-compatibility mode support
- Secure Shell (SSH) protocol support in the Administration Console (*Answer C*)
- Ability to establish a secure connection without a password in Design Studio (*Answer D*)

Question 4

The correct answer is **B**. No value is assigned to the PCKCACHESZ database configuration parameter when the value ANALYTICS is assigned to the DB2_WORKLOAD registry variable.

Instead, when the value ANALYTICS is assigned to the DB2_WORKLOAD registry variable:

- The DFT_TABLE_ORG database configuration parameter is set to COLUMN.
- The DFT_DEGREE database configuration parameter is set to ANY.

- The PAGESIZE database configuration parameter is set to 32 KB.

- The DFT_EXTENT_SZ database configuration parameter is set to 4.

- The INTRA_PARALLEL database manager configuration parameter is set to YES.

- The values of the SORTHEAP (*Answer A*) and SHEAPTHRES_SHR (*Answer D*) database configuration parameters are calculated and set specifically for an analytics workload.

- The UTIL_HEAP_SZ (*Answer C*) database configuration parameter is set to a value that takes into account the additional memory that is required to load data into column-organized tables.

- The AUTO_REORG database configuration parameter is set to ON.

- A default space reclamation policy is installed and automatic table maintenance is configured so that empty extents for column-organized tables are automatically returned to table space storage for reuse.

Question 5

The correct answer is **D**. When the value ANALYTICS is assigned to the DB2_WORKLOAD registry variable, the DFT_EXTENT_SZ database configuration parameter is set to 4.

On the other hand, when the value ANALYTICS is assigned to the DB2_WORKLOAD registry variable, the PAGESIZE database configuration parameter is set to 32 KB (*Answer A*), the DFT_DEGREE database configuration parameter is set to ANY (*Answer B*), and the UTIL_HEAP_SZ (*Answer C*) database configuration parameter is set to a value that takes into account the additional memory that is required to load data into column-organized tables.

Question 6

The correct answer is **A**. When the DB2_WORKLOAD registry variable is set to ANALYTICS, a default space reclamation policy is installed and automatic table maintenance is configured so that empty extents are automatically returned to table space storage for reuse whenever data is deleted from column-organized tables.

The AUTO_REORG (*Answer B*) and AUTO_TBL_MAINT (*Answer C*) database configuration parameters can only be assigned the values ON or OFF, and by default, a storage group named IBMSTOGROUP—not IBMUSRSTOGROUP (*Answer D*)—is created whenever a new DB2 10.5 database is created and all table spaces are assigned to this storage group. However, this storage group has nothing to do with space reclamation.

Question 7

The correct answer is **A**. When the DB2_WORKLOAD registry variable is set to ANALYTICS, the INTRA_PARALLEL (use intrapartition query parallelism) database manager configuration parameter is set to YES. This turns intrapartition parallelism on at the instance level; however, this behavior does not take effect until the instance is stopped and restarted.

Stopping and restarting the database (*Answer B*) has no effect on intrapartition parallelism; nor does dropping and recreating existing row-organized (*Answer C*) and column-organized (*Answer D*) tables.

Question 8

The correct answers are **C** and **E**. To aid in concurrency control, a SYSDEFAULTMANAGEDSUBCLASS service subclass workload management object is created automatically (under the SYSDEFAULTUSERCLASS superclass) for new (or upgraded) DB2 10.5 databases. This is the service subclass where heavyweight queries against column-organized tables run and can be controlled and monitored as a group.

A workload is an object that is used to identify submitted database work or a user connection so it can be managed (*Answer A*). A work action set is an object that dictates what is to happen when the work of interest is detected (*Answer B*). And there is no service subclass that is used to control the number of lightweight queries that are running concurrently (*Answer D*).

Question 9

The correct answers are **A** and **D**. A SYSDEFAULTUSERWAS work action set workload management object is created automatically for new (or upgraded) DB2 10.5 databases. This work action set is enabled by default so that queries that meet the criteria specified for the SYSMANAGEDQUERIES work class run in the SYSDEFAULTMANAGEDSUBCLASS service subclass.

The SYSDEFAULTUSERWAS work action set is NOT disabled by default (*Answer B*), and there is no USRDEFAULTMANAGEDSUBCLASS service subclass (*Answer C* and *Answer E*).

Question 10

The correct answer is **B**. DB2 Warehouse is a suite of products that combines the strength of DB2 with a data warehousing infrastructure. However, DB2 Warehouse Gateway is not a component of this suite of products.

On the other hand, the following components *are* provided in DB2 Warehouse:

- DB2 Warehouse Data Server (*Answer C*)
- DB2 Warehouse Application Server (*Answer D*)
- DB2 Warehouse Client (*Answer A*)

Physical Design

Question 11

The correct answer is **C**. When the majority of database workloads are entirely analytical or OLAP in nature, the recommended approach is to put as many tables as possible into column-organized format. Analytical and OLAP workloads are typically characterized by nonselective data access—usually involving more than 5 percent of the data—and extensive scanning, grouping, and aggregation.

When the majority of database workloads are transactional in nature, it is recommended that traditional row-organized tables (*Answer B*) be used; in this case, the use of column-organized tables should be avoided. Materialized query tables (*Answer D*) are used primarily to improve the performance of queries. And shadow tables (*Answer A*) offer a way to get the query performance benefits provided by BLU Acceleration in an online transaction processing (OLTP) environment.

Question 12

The correct answer is **B**. When the majority of database workloads are transactional in nature, it is recommended that traditional row-organized tables (with index access) be used; here, the use of column-organized tables should be avoided.

When the majority of database workloads are entirely analytical or OLAP in nature, the recommended approach is to put as many tables as possible into column-organized format (*Answer C*). Materialized query tables (*Answer D*) are used primarily to improve the performance of queries. And shadow tables (*Answer A*) offer a way to get the query performance benefits provided by BLU Acceleration in an online transaction processing (OLTP) environment.

Question 13

The correct answers are **C** and **E**. DB2 10.5 with BLU Acceleration was designed around the following seven "big ideas":

1. Simple to implement and use

2. Compute-friendly approximate Huffman encoding and compression

3. Multiply the power of the CPU (by taking advantage of SIMD)

4. Column data store

5. Core-friendly parallelism

6. Scan-friendly memory caching that improves buffer pool utilization

7. Data skipping

Adaptive row compression is neither "always on" nor is it part of BLU Acceleration (*Answer A*); although referential integrity informational constraints have been available for quite some time, default informational constraints are not supported (*Answer B*); and while the use of BLU Acceleration can result in a smaller storage footprint for data, the same cannot be said for transaction logs (*Answer D*).

Question 14

The correct answer is **D**. For mixed workloads, which include a combination of analytic query processing and very selective data access (involving less than 2 percent of the data), it can be beneficial to use a mixture of row-organized and column-organized tables, as opposed to just one table type.

When the majority of database workloads are transactional in nature, it is recommended that traditional row-organized tables (with index access) be used (*Answer A*). When the majority of database workloads are entirely analytical or OLAP in nature, the recommended approach is to put as many tables as possible into column-organized format (*Answer B*). Analytical and OLAP workloads are typically characterized by nonselective data access—usually involving more than 5 percent of the data—and extensive scanning, grouping, and aggregation (*Answer C*).

Question 15

The correct answer is **C**. In most cases, column-organized tables can be referenced in the same way that row-organized tables can. For example, both types of tables can serve as the source or target of a view—provided the view is not created with the `WITH CHECK OPTION` clause specified.

There are some instances, however, where column-organized tables cannot be used. For example, they cannot be referenced as the source or target of an index (*Answer A*), a trigger (*Answer B*), or a nickname (*Answer D*).

Question 16

The correct answer is **B**. When column-organized tables are used, REORGs do not have to be manually performed—*they're done automatically.*

Column-organized tables can only be created in automatic storage databases (*Answer C*). Column-organized tables differ from row-organized tables in the following ways:

- Indexes are not needed, nor can they be created
- Multidimensional clustering is not needed, nor is it allowed
- Materialized query tables, materialized views, and statistical views are not needed, nor are they allowed
- Table partitioning is not supported (*Answer A*)

In addition, column-organized tables cannot be created if the DB2_ COMPATIBILITY_VECTOR registry variable has been assigned the value ORA (to enable Oracle-compatibility) (*Answer D*).

Question 17

The correct answer is **A**. Value compression optimizes space usage by removing duplicate entries for a value, and only storing one copy of the data—the stored copy keeps track of the location of all other references to the data value. In addition, when value compression is used, NULLs and zero-length data that has been assigned to columns with variable-length data types (i.e., VARCHAR, VARGRAPHIC, BLOB, CLOB, and DBCLOB) are not stored on disk.

With approximate Huffman encoding (also referred to as actionable compression), values that appear more frequently are compressed at a higher level than values that do not appear as often (*Answer B*). Row compression is applied by searching for repeating patterns in the data and replacing those patterns with 12-bit symbols, which are stored along with the patterns they represent in a table-level or page-level dictionary (*Answer C*). And with backup compression, all of the data in the backup image, including catalog tables, index objects, LOB objects, and database metadata, is compressed (almost, but not quite *Answer D*).

Question 18

The correct answer is **C**. While row and actionable compression work on a table-by-table basis, when backup compression is used, all of the data in the backup image, including catalog tables, index objects, LOB objects, and database metadata, is compressed. And it makes no difference if data and index objects are stored in the same table space or in different table spaces.

Backup compression and row compression can be used together to minimize backup image sizes (*Answer A*). However, the use of backup compression requires additional CPU resources and can lengthen the time it takes to perform a backup operation (*Answer B*). Table compression alone can significantly reduce backup storage space requirements; therefore, if row compression is utilized, backup compression should only be used if a reduction in backup storage space is more important than shorter backup times (*Answer D*).

Question 19

The correct answer is **B**. With adaptive row compression, there can be one table-level compression dictionary and multiple page-level compression dictionaries for each table that gets compressed; each page-level dictionary contains a mapping of patterns that frequently occur in rows throughout a single page.

Before data in a table can be compressed, the table must be "enabled" for compression (*Answer A*). When a table is enabled for adaptive compression, the entire table is enabled, even if it is a partitioned table that consists of multiple data partitions (*Answer C*). And when a database is converted to DB2 10.5, existing compressed tables will have classic row compression enabled; current and future records will be compressed at the table level (*Answer D*).

Question 20

The correct answer is **C**. When an existing index is enabled for compression, its data will automatically be compressed—no additional steps are required. (If the associated table is REORGed, a new table-level compression dictionary may be built for the table, but index compression is not dependent upon a new table-level compression dictionary being built.)

Before data in an index can be compressed, the index must be enabled for compression; this is done by executing either the CREATE INDEX ... COMPRESS YES or the ALTER INDEX [*IndexName*] COMPRESS YES statement. The ALTER INDEX statement can also be used to disable an index for compression (*Answer A*). Index compression is automatically enabled for compressed tables and automatically disabled for uncompressed tables (*Answer B*). And The following types of indexes can NOT be enabled for compression (*Answer D*):

- Multidimensional clustering (MDC) block indexes
- Insert time clustering (ITC) block indexes
- Catalog indexes
- XML indexes
- Indexes on created global temporary tables
- Indexes on declared global temporary tables

Question 21

The correct answers are **A** and **E**. An expression-based index is an index whose key is derived from some type of expression; for example, a scalar function. When the UNIQUE clause is specified in the CREATE INDEX statement used to create an expression-based index, uniqueness will be enforced against the values stored in the index—not the values stored in the associated table.

Expression-based indexes are best suited for queries that contain some type of column expression, not a sequence (*Answer B*) or a user-defined function (*Answer C*). When an expression-based index is created, two supporting objects are created as well: *a system-generated package* and *a system-generated statistical view*. The package is used to generate key values while the statistical view is used for statistics collection—when the RUNSTATS command is issued against a table for which one or more expression-based indexes have been defined, statistics for the expression-based keys are collected and stored in the corresponding statistical view (*Answer D*).

Question 22

The correct answer is **C**. When an expression-based index is created, two supporting objects are created as well: *a system-generated package* and *a system-generated statistical view*.

Aliases (*Answer A*) and triggers (*Answer B*) are user-defined objects; i.e., they are NOT created automatically to support other objects. A synopsis table (*Answer D*) is a system-generated, column-organized table that BLU Acceleration uses to store the minimum and maximum range of the data values found in "chunks" of data records that are stored in a user-defined, column-organized table; when an analytic query is executed, BLU Acceleration uses the information stored in synopsis tables to skip over data that is of no interest.

Question 23

The correct answer is **D**. When the RUNSTATS command is issued against a table for which one or more expression-based indexes have been defined, statistics for the expression-based keys are collected and stored in a corresponding statistical view.

The definition of an index is stored in the system catalog (*Answer A*). A synopsis table (*Answer B*) is a system-generated, column-organized table that BLU Acceleration uses to store the minimum and maximum range of the data values found in "chunks" of data records that are stored in a user-defined, column-organized table; when an analytic query is executed, BLU Acceleration uses the information stored in synopsis tables to skip over data that is of no interest. And, a summary table (*Answer C*) is a special type of a materialized query table (MQT) that specifically includes summary data. DB2 Warehouse uses summary tables to improve the performance of queries issued to cube models and cubes.

Question 24

The correct answer is **A**. Expression-based indexes are created by executing the CREATE INDEX statement with one or more expressions specified. For example, when executed, the following SQL statement:

```
CREATE INDEX emp_name_idx ON employee(UPPER(name))
```

will create an expression-based index named EMP_NAME_IDX whose key values consist of values retrieved from a column named NAME in a table named EMPLOYEE that have been converted to upper case.

There is no CREATE EXPRESSION BASED INDEX statement (*Answer D*), and the CREATE INDEX statement does not have an EXPRESSION clause (*Answer B* and *Answer C*).

Question 25

The correct answer is **A**. Prior to DB2 10.5, only check and referential integrity constraints could be created as informational constraints. Starting with DB2 10.5, primary key and unique informational constraints can be created as well. However, NOT NULL and default constraints cannot be created as informational constraints.

An informational constraint is a constraint that is used to provide the DB2 optimizer with information that may help improve query performance, but that is not enforced (*Answer D*). Informational constraints are defined by appending the keywords NOT ENFORCED to primary key, unique, check, and referential integrity constraint definitions (*Answer C*). And, while indexes cannot be created for column-organized tables, informational primary keys and informational unique constraints can (*Answer B*).

Question 26

The correct answer is **C**. If extended row size support is enabled, whenever a row is inserted or updated in a table and the physical length of the data for the row exceeds the maximum record length allowed (by the underlying table space), a subset of the data stored in a varying-length string column is moved out of the row and stored as large object (LOB) data (*Answer D*). When this happens, the varying-length string column's data type does NOT change (i.e., the column's data type is NOT converted to CLOB or DBCLOB).

Extended row size support is enabled by assigning the value ENABLE to the EXTENDED_ROW_SZ database configuration parameter (*Answer B*). And, to take advantage of extended row size support, a table must have at least one column with a varying-length string data type (*Answer A*).

Question 27

The correct answer is **B**. Normally, records in a table are organized into pages that are 4, 8, 16, or 32 KB in length. And with versions prior to DB2 10.5 (as well as with DB2 10.5 if extended row size support is not enabled), the maximum number of bytes allowed in a single row is dependent upon the page size of the table space being used to store the table.

While the page size of the database (*Answer A*) does determine the page size that is used by the default user table space (USERSPACE1), it is the page size of the table space and not the page size of the database that determines the maximum length allowed for a record. There is no DB2_DEFAULT_ROW_SIZE registry variable (*Answer C*); there is no MAX_ROW_SZ database configuration parameter (*Answer D*), either.

Question 28

The correct answers are **D** and **E**. An index for which entries will not be made when all parts of the index key contain the NULL value can be created by executing a CREATE INDEX statement with the EXCLUDE NULL KEYS clause specified. If such an index is defined as being unique (by also specifying the UNIQUE clause with the CREATE INDEX statement used), rows with NULL key values are not used to enforce uniqueness.

Although the resulting index *will* require less storage space, it will also be more efficient—not less efficient (*Answer A*). The CREATE INDEX statement will NOT fail (*Answer B*), and it will NOT return a warning because the UNIQUE clause and the EXCLUDE NULL KEYS clause can be used together (*Answer C*).

Monitoring DB2 Activity

Question 29

The correct answer is **D**. The POOL_COL_L_READS monitoring element keeps track of the number of column-organized pages that were requested from a buffer pool (logical) for regular and large table spaces.

The POOL_COL_LBP_PAGES_FOUND monitoring element keeps track of the number of times that a column-organized page was present in a local buffer pool (*Answer A*). The OBJECT_COL_L_READS monitoring element keeps track of the number of column-organized pages that were logically read from a buffer pool for a table (*Answer B*). And the OBJECT_COL_LBP_PAGES_FOUND monitoring element keeps track of the number of times that a column-organized page for a table was present in a local buffer pool (*Answer C*).

Question 30

The correct answer is **B**. The SKIPPED_PREFETCH_COL_P_READS monitoring element keeps track of the number of column-organized pages that an I/O server (prefetcher) skipped because they were already loaded into a buffer pool.

There is no SKIPPED_PREFETCH_COL_L_READS monitoring element (*Answer A*) or SKIPPED_PREFETCH_UOW_COL_L_READS monitoring element (*Answer C*). And the SKIPPED_PREFETCH_UOW_COL_P_READS monitoring element keeps track of the number of column-organized pages that an I/O server (prefetcher) skipped because they were already loaded into a buffer pool *by an agent in the same unit of work* (*Answer D*).

Question 31

The correct answer is **B**. The POOL_ASYNC_COL_READS monitoring element keeps track of the number of column-organized pages read in from table space containers (physical) by a prefetcher (for regular and large table spaces).

The OBJECT_COL_P_READS monitoring element keeps track of the number of column-organized pages that were physically read from a buffer pool for a table (*Answer A*). The POOL_ASYNC_COL_READS monitoring element keeps track of the number of column-organized pages read in from table space containers (physical) by a prefetcher for regular and large table spaces (*Answer C*). And the POOL_ASYNC_COL_READ_REQS monitoring element keeps track of the number of asynchronous column-organized read requests made by the prefetcher to the operating system (*Answer D*).

Question 32

The correct answer is **D**. The SKIPPED_PREFETCH_UOW_COL_P_READS monitoring element keeps track of the number of column-organized pages that an I/O server (prefetcher) skipped because they were already loaded into a buffer pool by an agent in the same unit of work (transaction).

There is no SKIPPED_PREFETCH_COL_L_READS monitoring element (*Answer A*) or SKIPPED_PREFETCH_UOW_COL_L_READS monitoring element (*Answer C*). And the SKIPPED_PREFETCH_COL_P_READS monitoring element keeps track of the number of column-organized pages that an I/O server (prefetcher) skipped because they were already loaded into a buffer pool (*Answer B*).

Question 33

The correct answer is **C**. New to DB2 10.5, the Columnar Table Queue (CTQ) operator is used in an Explain access plan to represent the transition between column-organized data processing and row-organized data processing.

There is no Row Transition Queue (*Answer B*) or Columnar Transition Queue (*Answer D*) operator. And table queues (which are also referred to as row-table queues) are used to move data between subsections in a partitioned database environment or between subagents in a symmetric multiprocessor (SMP) environment (*Answer A*).

Question 34

The correct answer is **D**. Starting with DB2 10.5, the OBJECT_TYPE column of the EXPLAIN_OBJECT table can contain the value "CO," which is a two-character descriptive label that indicates the record is for a column-organized table.

The columns OBJECT_COL_L_READS and OBJECT_COL_P_READS were added to the OBJECT_METRICS table in DB2 10.5—*not the EXPLAIN_OBJECT table* (*Answer A*). Values assigned to the ARGUMENT_TYPE and ARGUMENT_VALUE columns of the EXPLAIN_ARGUMENT table—*not the EXPLAIN_OBJECT table*—can indicate that a Columnar Table Queue (CTQ) operator is being used to transfer data from column-organized processing to row-organized processing (*Answer B*). And there is no db2exmig command (*Answer C*).

Question 35

The correct answer is **D**. The MON_GET_PKG_CACHE_STMT() monitoring table function returns a point-in-time view of both static and dynamic SQL statements in the database package cache, which can reveal how many rows have been written to or read from a column-organized table.

The MON_GET_TABLE_USAGE_LIST() monitoring table function returns information from a usage list that has been defined for a table (*Answer A*). There is no single monitoring table function that can be used to determine how many rows are returned from *all* tables in response to a particular query (*Answer B*). And the MON_GET_ACTIVITY() monitoring table function returns a list of all activities that were submitted by the specified application that have not yet been completed. (*Answer C*).

Question 36

The correct answer is **C**. The TOTAL_HASH_GRPBYS monitoring element keeps track of the total number of hashed GROUP BY operations that are performed. And because GROUP BY operations on column-organized tables use hashing as the grouping method, this monitoring element can be used to help tune database workloads that consist of queries that perform GROUP BY operations against column-organized tables.

The ACTIVE_HASH_GRPBYS monitoring element keeps track of the number of GROUP BY operations using hashing as their grouping method that are currently running and consuming sort heap memory (*Answer A*). The HASH_GRPBY_OVERFLOWS monitoring element keeps track of the number of times that GROUP BY operations using hashing as their grouping method exceeded the sort heap memory available (*Answer B*). And there is no monitoring element that can be used to reduce the amount time spent processing data for queries that access row- and column-organized tables (*Answer D*).

Question 37

The correct answers are **C** and **E**. The MON_GET_ACTIVITY_DETAILS() monitoring table function retrieves metrics about an activity, including general activity information and a set of metrics for the activity, and returns the data collected in an XML document. And the MON_GET_UNIT_OF_WORK_DETAILS() monitoring table function retrieves metrics for one or more transactions and returns the information in an XML document.

Essentially, any monitoring table function that has the word "DETAILS" in its name will return the information collected in an XML document; any monitoring table function that does NOT have this word as part of its name (*Answer A*, *Answer B*, and *Answer D*) will return the information collected in the form of a table.

Question 38

The correct answers are **A** and **D**. With DB2 10.5, the DB2 Problem Determination Tool can be used to monitor an HADR environment; the -hadr option is used with the db2pd command to indicate that HADR information is to be collected. The following new columns were also added to the result table produced by the MON_GET_HADR() monitor table function:

- **HADR_FLAGS**: A space-delimited string containing one or more flags that describe the current state of the HADR environment.

- **STANDBY_SPOOL_PERCENT**: Percentage of spool space used, relative to the configured spool limit. When the spool percentage reaches 100 percent, the standby database will stop receiving logs until space is released as replay proceeds. Spooling can stop before the limit is reached if the standby log path becomes full.

There is no EVMON_HADR_PSCALE procedure (*Answer B*), MON_HADR_UTILIZATION administrative view (*Answer C*), or SNAP_GET_HADR() monitoring table function (*Answer E*).

High Availability

Question 39

The correct answers are **B** and **D**. The following restrictions apply when HADR is used in a DB2 pureScale environment:

- The synchronous (SYNC) and near synchronous (NEARSYNC) synchronization modes are not supported

- Only one HADR standby database is allowed; multiple standbys are not supported.

- "Peer windows" do not exist.

- The "reads on standby" feature is not supported.

- Network address translation (NAT) between primary and standby sites is not supported.

- The primary and standby clusters must have the same member topology; that is, each instance must have the same number of DB2 members and each member must have the same member ID.

- The primary and standby clusters must have the same number of cluster caching facilities (CFs).
- IBM's Tivoli System Automation for Multi-Platforms (SA MP) cannot be used to manage automatic failover. (SA MP is responsible for managing high availability within the local cluster only.)

With HADR, two types of takeover operations can be performed. They are: role switch (*Answer A*) and failover. Only asynchronous (ASYNC) and super asynchronous (SUPERASYNC) synchronization modes can be used (*Answer E*). And in a DB2 pureScale - HADR environment, only one member of the standby cluster replays logs; all other members remain inactive. Members in the primary cluster ship their logs to the replay member at the standby using a TCP connection; the replay member merges and replays the log streams. If the standby cannot connect to a particular member on the primary, another member on the primary (that the standby can connect to) sends the logs for the unconnected member. This is known as assisted remote catchup (*Answer C*).

Question 40

The correct answer is **A**. An HADR role switch is initiated by executing the TAKEOVER HADR command (from any member of the standby cluster) and can only be performed when the primary is available.

An HADR failover is initiated by executing the TAKEOVER HADR BY FORCE command (*Answer B*) from any member of the standby cluster—not from the Cluster Caching Facility (*Answer C* and *Answer D*)—and can only be performed when the primary is unavailable.

Question 41

The correct answers are **B** and **E**. The following restrictions apply when HADR is used in a DB2 pureScale environment:

- The synchronous (SYNC) and near synchronous (NEARSYNC) synchronization modes are not supported
- Only one HADR standby database is allowed; multiple standbys are not supported.
- "Peer windows" do not exist.
- The "reads on standby" feature is not supported.
- Network address translation (NAT) between primary and standby sites is not supported.

- The primary and standby clusters must have the same member topology; that is, each instance must have the same number of DB2 members and each member must have the same member ID.

- The primary and standby clusters must have the same number of cluster caching facilities (CFs).

- IBM's Tivoli System Automation for Multi-Platforms (SA MP) cannot be used to manage automatic failover. (SA MP is responsible for managing high availability within the local cluster only.)

The primary and standby clusters are NOT required to have the same number of CPUs (*Answer A*), the same amount of storage (*Answer C*), or the same amount of memory (*Answer D*).

Question 42

The correct answers are **A** and **C**. With DB2 10.5, it's possible to restore a database backup image taken on one DB2 pureScale instance to another DB2 pureScale instance that has a different topology. However, a common member must be present in both the source and target DB2 pureScale instances.

Although a common member must be present in both the source and target DB2 pureScale instances in order to restore a database backup image taken on one DB2 pureScale instance to another DB2 pureScale instance that has a different topology, the two instances are not required to share the same storage (*Answer B*) or the same high-speed interconnect network (*Answer D*). Similarly, a common cluster caching facility (CF) does not have to be present in both the source and target pureScale systems (*Answer E*).

Question 43

The correct answer is **D**. With DB2 10.5, the addition of new members no longer requires an offline database backup to be taken before cataloged databases are marked "usable."

New members can be added to a DB2 pureScale instance while the instance remains online and accessible (*Answer B*). As before, new members are added to a DB2 pureScale cluster by executing the db2iupdt command (*Answer A*). And cataloged databases are available on the new member immediately upon the successful completion of this command (*Answer C*).

Question 44

The correct answer is **B**. To create an index that uses random ordering for index key storage, you supply the RANDOM clause with the key column definition that is specified in a CREATE INDEX statement. For example:

```
CREATE INDEX dept_idx ON department(dept_id RANDOM)
```

There is no CREATE RANDOM INDEX statement.

Random ordering on index key columns helps to alleviate page contention on frequently accessed pages in certain INSERT scenarios (*Answer D*). When values are stored at random places in the index tree, the number of consecutive insertions on a page decreases (*Answer C*). This alleviates page contention, particularly in DB2 pureScale environments where pages are shared between DB2 members (*Answer D*). And index key column values that are stored in random order can be used in non-matching index scans (*Answer A*). Index-only access on random key columns is also possible.

Question 45

The correct answer is **C**. Beginning with DB2 10.5, FixPack 1, it is possible to isolate application workloads to one or more specific members that have been assigned to a member subset (i.e., multi-tenancy). By using member subsets, batch processing can be isolated from transactional workloads and multiple databases within a single instance can be separated from one another.

Prior to DB2 10.5, an application could either be configured to run on a single member of a DB2 pureScale cluster (referred to as *client affinity*) (*Answer B*) or across all of the cluster members (known as *workload balancing*) (*Answer A*)—there were no other options. Multi-tenancy has nothing to do with the types of workloads that can be run in a DB2 pureScale environment (*Answer D*).

Question 46

The correct answer is **C**. Starting with DB2 10.5, it is possible to apply FixPack updates to a DB2 pureScale environment while the DB2 instance remains available; this is done by applying the update to one database server at a time while the remaining database servers continue to process transactions. (Immediately after a database server has been updated, it can resume transaction processing.)

The db2iupdt command is used to add new members to a DB2 pureScale cluster—not to apply FixPacks (*Answer A*). To apply a FixPack in previous releases, the DB2 pureScale instance had to be taken offline, but that is no longer the case (*Answer B*). And, a database backup operation does NOT have to be performed immediately after a DB2 pureScale database server has been updated (*Answer D*).

Question 47

The correct answers are **B** and **C**. DB2 Advanced Copy Services (ACS) allows the fast copying technology of a storage device to be used to perform the data copying task of backup and restore operations. (A backup image that is created with DB2 ACS is known as a "snapshot" backup.) With DB2 10.5, if you want to perform snapshot operations on a storage device that doesn't have a vendor-supplied DB2 ACS API driver, you can do so by creating a DB2 ACS script. Three types of DB2 ACS scripts can exist:

- **Snapshot backup**: Performs the actions needed to create a snapshot backup image.
- **Snapshot restore**: Performs the actions needed to restore a database from a snapshot backup image.
- **Snapshot management**: Performs the actions needed to delete a snapshot backup image.

And a snapshot restore script can execute the following actions:

- **prepare**: Runs any actions that need to take place before the snapshot restore operation is performed.
- **restore**: Performs the snapshot restore operation.

A snapshot *backup* script can execute the following actions instead:

- **prepare**: Runs any actions that need to take place before the snapshot backup operation is performed.
- **snapshot**: Performs the snapshot backup operation.
- **verify**: Verifies that a snapshot backup image was successfully produced (*Answer A*).
- **rollback**: Cleans up the backup image if the snapshot operation fails (*Answer D*).
- **store_metadata**: Specifies actions that can occur after a snapshot backup image has been produced and all required metadata has been written to a protocol file (*Answer E*).

Question 48

The correct answer is **B**. DB2 ACS scripts work in conjunction with DB2 ACS protocol files, which are created by the DB2 ACS library and contain information that is needed to perform snapshot backup operations. A DB2 ACS protocol file is divided into different sections, each of which shows the progress and options of each DB2 ACS API function call. The data in each section contains, among other things, *any commands that were used to invoke the script*—NOT the commands the DB2 ACS script invoked.

Specifically, the data in each section of a DB2 ACS protocol file contains the following information:

- The DB2 ACS API function name (*Answer A*)
- The beginning and ending timestamp for when the function started and ended (*Answer D*)
- Commands that were used to invoke the script
- Any options that were provided with the function call (*Answer C*)

Utilities

Question 49

The correct answer is **C**. IBM InfoSphere Optim pureQuery Runtime—*NOT Optim Query Tuner Workflow Assistant*—provides a runtime environment and application programming interface (API) that enhances the performance, security, and manageability of database client applications.

Optim Query Tuner Workflow Assistant is a Data Studio GUI interface for IBM InfoSphere Optim Query Workload Tuner (*Answer A*) that can be used to format an SQL query such that each table reference, each column reference, and each predicate is presented on its own line, which can be expanded to drill down into the parts of a query so its structure can be better understood (*Answer D*). And before the Optim Query Tuner Workflow Assistant will collect new Explain information for the same SQL statement, the catalog cache must be updated (*Answer B*).

Question 50

The correct answer is **D**. The Workload Access Plan Comparison feature of the Optim Workload Table Organization Advisor can be used to fix or compare data access plans. Using this tool, the access plans from two Explain snapshots can be compared to validate Query Workload Tuner recommendations. To make such a comparison, Explain data would need to be generated for the original queries, the workload would then need to be tuned, Explain data would then have to be generated for the new queries, and finally both sets of Explain data would need to be compared.

IBM InfoSphere Optim Performance Manager provides information that can help identify, diagnose, solve, and proactively prevent performance problems (*Answer A*). IBM InfoSphere Optim Query Workload Tuner provides expert recommendations to help improve the performance of SQL queries and query workloads (*Answer B*). And IBM InfoSphere Optim Query Tuner Workflow Assistant is a Data Studio GUI interface that can be used to format an SQL query such that each table reference, each column reference, and each predicate is presented on its own line, which can be expanded to drill down into the parts of a query so its structure can be better understood (*Answer C*).

Question 51

The correct answers are **A** and **C**. IBM InfoSphere Optim Query Workload Tuner provides expert recommendations to help improve the performance of SQL queries and query workloads. With the full-featured, licensed version, this tool will also generate the DDL needed to create or modify indexes that can improve performance.

IBM InfoSphere Optim Performance Manager provides information that can help identify, diagnose, solve, and proactively prevent performance problems (*Answer B*). The full-featured, licensed version of IBM InfoSphere Optim Query Workload Tuner does NOT create reports that summarize the statistics the DB2 optimizer uses to generate data access plans (*Answer D*). And IBM InfoSphere Data Architect provides a collaborative data design solution that enables you to discover, model, standardize, and integrate diverse and distributed queries (*Answer E*).

Question 52

The correct answer is **D**. A load operation has several distinct phases; they are, in order:

- Analyze
- Load
- Build
- Delete
- Index copy

The Index copy phase is only used when row-organized tables are loaded. The Analyze phase (*Answer C*), the Load phase, the Build phase (*Answer A*), and the Delete phase (*Answer B*) are used when data is loaded into column-organized tables.

Question 53

The correct answer is **B**. A load operation has several distinct phases; they are, in order:

- Analyze
- Load
- Build
- Delete
- Index copy

The Analyze phase is only used when data is loaded into column-organized tables; the Index copy phase is only used when row-organized tables are loaded. So, the correct order of the phases that are used when data is loaded into a row-organized table are: Load, Build, Delete, and Index copy.

The correct order of the phases that are used when data is loaded into a column-organized table are: Analyze, Load, Build, and Delete (*Answer A*). Any other combination (*Answer C* and *Answer D*) is incorrect.

Question 54

The correct answer is **A**. During the Analyze phase, a column compression dictionary is built, if needed (which is the case if a LOAD REPLACE, LOAD REPLACE RESETDICTIONARY, or LOAD REPLACE RESETDICTIONARYONLY operation is performed; this is also the case if a LOAD INSERT operation is performed against an empty column-organized table).

During the Load phase (*Answer B*), data is loaded into the table, and index keys and table statistics are collected, if appropriate. During the Build phase (*Answer C*), indexes are produced based on the index keys collected during the Load phase. And during the Delete phase (*Answer D*), rows that violated a unique or primary key are removed from the table.

Question 55

The correct answer is **C**. The STATISTICS USE PROFILE option and the NONRECOVERABLE option of the LOAD command are not mutually exclusive—they can be used together.

The STATISTICS USE PROFILE option is disabled, by default, for column-organized tables (*Answer A*). (Instead, the STATISTICS NO option is enabled, by default, for row-organized tables.) The STATISTICS USE PROFILE option is enabled, by default, for column-organized tables (*Answer B*). And a statistics profile should exist before the STATISTICS USE PROFILE option is used; but, if a profile doesn't exist, statistics will be collected using the default options that are used to perform automatic RUNSTATS operations (*Answer D*).

Question 56

The correct answer is **B**. The -stopBeforeSwap parameter is used with the db2convert command to specify that the db2convert utility is to stop before performing the SWAP phase of the ADMIN_MOVE_TABLE() procedure and prompt the user to perform an online backup operation before continuing.

The -check parameter specifies that conversion notes are to be generated and displayed, but that the actual conversion process is not to take place (*Answer A*). There is no -pauseForBackup parameter for the db2convert command (*Answer C*). And the -opt COPY_USE_LOAD parameter specifies that the ADMIN_MOVE_TABLE() procedure is to copy the data by default (*Answer D*).

Notes

Notes

Notes

Notes